What's a Parent to Do?

What's a Parent to Do?

How to Give Your Child the Best Education

Lawrence Baines

ROWMAN & LITTLEFIELD
Lanham • Boulder • New York • London

Published by Rowman & Littlefield
An imprint of The Rowman & Littlefield Publishing Group, Inc.
4501 Forbes Boulevard, Suite 200, Lanham, Maryland 20706
www.rowman.com

86-90 Paul Street, London EC2A 4NE, United Kingdom

Copyright © 2022 by Lawrence Baines

All rights reserved. No part of this book may be reproduced in any form or by any electronic or mechanical means, including information storage and retrieval systems, without written permission from the publisher, except by a reviewer who may quote passages in a review.

British Library Cataloguing in Publication Information Available

Library of Congress Cataloging-in-Publication Data Available

ISBN 9781475866780 (cloth : alk. paper) | ISBN 9781475866797 (pbk. : alk. paper) | ISBN 9781475866803 (epub)

"If America stands for anything, it stands for the principle that all men are created equal or, at least, that they should have an equal opportunity at birth to reach as far as they wish to."—George B. Kaiser

Mr. Kaiser has given millions of dollars and countless hours of his life to enhancing the education and quality of life for all children.

This book is dedicated to him.

Contents

Preface	ix
Acknowledgments	xi
Introduction: The Enduring Benefits of a Good Education	xiii

PART I: AT HOME — 1

1	Make Home Not Only Loving and Safe But Also Fun and Interesting	3
2	Pay Attention	9
3	Have Plenty of Print Materials and Toys on Hand	13
4	Limit Screen Time	17
5	Get Moving and Get Outside	21
6	Engage with the Arts	25
7	Help Your Child Choose a Musical Instrument	29
8	Seek Out Diverse Experiences	33
9	Promote Resilience	37

PART II: AT SCHOOL — 41

10	Choose the Best School	43
	10a For Public Schools, Follow the Money	47
	10b For Private Schools, Do Your Due Diligence	56
	10c Avoid Charter Schools	61

11	Select the Right Teacher	65
	11a Actively Seek Out the Best	68
	11b Insist on Honesty and Enthusiasm	70
	11c Consider the Teacher's Education and Experience	74
12	Get into Gifted	79
13	Encourage Participation in Noncontact Sports; No Team Sports Before Age Ten	85
14	Take Advantage of School Services	91
15	Attend School Events	97
Notes		101
About the Author		137

Preface

Making School and Home Work for Your Child

My job as a professor of education requires me to continually stay up-to-date with the latest research on learning. I routinely navigate through stacks of academic studies, statistical jargon, and neuroscientific investigations with the goal of finding the most beneficial insights. My career has been built around translating findings from research into practical strategies for parents and teachers.

I have written a dozen books and 100+ articles and made hundreds of presentations, and the theme has been the same—how to optimize the education of children. Because of the ubiquity of standardized testing, many Americans today equate the term "education" with test scores. This book is not about how to optimize the test scores of children. Rather, *education* is construed as the *Oxford English Dictionary* defines it: "The process of bringing up a child, with reference to forming character, shaping manners and behavior."[1]

One of the great benefits of working in education is that I also get to spend a lot of time in schools, and I get to see firsthand how policies, new instructional strategies, and cultural trends play out "in real life" with "real children." After working in hundreds of schools, I have gotten to the point where I can walk into any school in the country and, within two minutes of entering the front door, offer an accurate assessment of the school's quality. I can get a sense of the competence of a teacher almost as quickly.

While my particular talent for identifying great schools and accomplished teachers may not generate much envy (or money), it has come in handy repeatedly when moving from one house, school, and teacher to another. Some aspects of the American system of schooling are unfair; many aspects are truly bizarre. My objective with this book is not to assess the fairness of the system but to explain how to work effectively within it.

I offer no guarantee that, if you follow the suggestions in the book, your child will grow up to be a happy, healthy genius. However, I can confidently assert that if you follow the suggestions in this book, the probability of raising a happy, healthy genius will increase substantially.

Acknowledgments

What's a Parent to Do?: How to Give Your Child the Best Education translates educational research into practical strategies for parents. I could not have finished this two-year project without immense help from friends and family.

I have many people to thank. With regard to the following:

1. Research—Sara Huffman, Dr. Jim Machell, Coleen Baines, Alex Krem, and David Ferguson;
2. Design, readability, and title—Dr. Jeremy Worsham, Morgan Upchurch, R. L. Baines, R. E. Baines, and Trevor Proctor;
3. Photography—Jack Baines and Andrew Crane;
4. Moral support—Dr. Gregg Garn, Dr. Sissi Carroll, Dr. Tom Gage, Kathryn Baines, Dr. Ed Farrell, Dr. Micah Dial, and Dr. Anthony Kunkel.

As studies cited in this book attest in countless ways, it is the loving support of family and friends that makes life worth living.

Introduction
The Enduring Benefits of a Good Education

The Federal Bureau of Investigation and the U.S. Attorney General's Office discovered that a group of rich parents had been bribing admissions officers and coaches at high-prestige universities so that their children could gain admission.[1] During 2019–2020, over fifty people were charged in the investigation, nicknamed Operation Varsity Blues, and some parents went to prison.

A national furor erupted over the idea that rich people might try to secure the best possible education for their children.[2] While bribery and deception are not particularly admirable traits, the impulse to want the best education for your child is not only understandable—it is human nature.

Perhaps parents trying to gain entrance for their children to prestigious universities had discovered the U.S. Department of Education database of degrees and compared the high salaries garnered by Ivy League grads against salaries garnered by graduates from other institutions. If so, they would have found out that the top 10 percent of Ivy League grads earned "$200,000 or more" after graduation while the top 10 percent from non-Ivy League schools earned less than $70,000.[3]

The connection between a high-quality education and a high salary has been well established.[4] In general, individuals who are more educated tend to make more money—a lot more. The average salary for someone who did not finish high school is $31,000; the average salary for someone with a bachelor's degree is $65,000, with a master's degree is $78,000, and with a doctoral degree is $98,000.[5] These differences in annual salary translate into millions of dollars over the course of a working life.

Experts expect differences in income due to educational attainment to grow exponentially over the next decade.[6] Those with only a high school diploma and those who did not graduate from high school will have few options and low wages.[7] At the same time, the well-educated will have numerous opportunities, meaning good jobs at generous salaries.[8]

The adage is that "money cannot buy happiness."[9] However, recent research has found that money can make you happ*ier*, at least in relative terms.[10] Although it is difficult to attribute shifts in attitude to a single phenomenon, research has found that people who have lots of money tend to be happier than people who have very little of it.[11]

Over twenty years ago, a group of economists got together and calculated that a monetary "sweet spot" exists for the achievement of happiness.[12] As one of the researchers noted, "Not having enough money to live a decent life really gets in the way of doing the ordinary things that make people happy."[13] For example, anxiety over bills due at the end of every month would disappear if sufficient funds were in the bank. In this way, money can act to alleviate stress and instill confidence.

The sweet spot in 2022 dollars is supposedly around $90,000.[14] Subsequent studies have found that while incomes above $90,000 might not translate into higher satisfaction, more money promotes a higher sense of "well-being."[15] So, while a billionaire may not have a better quality of life than the person who earns $90,000, the billionaire might have a thicker financial cushion and consequently, might spend less time worrying about the future.

In addition to higher salaries, employees with more education are typically the last to lose their jobs while those with the least education are among the first to get laid off.[16] Not only is a good education a smart choice financially, but it also has intrinsic benefits. As my wise Uncle Jack always said, "They can take away everything you have, but they can never take away what you know."

THE REAL WORLD

America was built on high ideals, "that all men are created equal, that they are endowed by their Creator with certain unalienable Rights, that among these are Life, Liberty and the pursuit of Happiness."[17] Despite good intentions, the benefits of American citizenship are not uniformly distributed. For some, the pursuit of happiness can be an enjoyable walk in the park; for others, it can be a soul-crushing nightmare. The system as it currently exists can seem unjust, callous, and capricious.

Horace Mann, the staunch advocate for universal, free public schools, wrote that education "is not only a moral renovator, and a multiplier of intellectual power, but that it is also the most prolific parent of material riches."[18]

Experts agree that the development of character, intellect, and future success is contingent upon the quality of a child's education.[19] The good news is that success or failure in education is almost always due to wholly controllable phenomena.

Knowing *how* to build a quality education is the key.

This book is divided into two parts: home and school, and suggests fifteen strategies. With knowledge of the fifteen strategies, any parent can provide their child with an exemplary education.

Part I

AT HOME

Strategy 1

Make Home Not Only Loving and Safe But Also Fun and Interesting

Home is the place where, when you have to go there, they have to take you in.[1]

For most people, home means more than simply not being turned away, but imagine if a person did not even have that assurance. Babies are still being abandoned at an alarming rate in the United States.[2] Worldwide, millions of young children are separated from their parents every year.[3] How would your life have been different if your parents had left you, unclaimed, at the hospital?[4] What if you had grown up having no place to call home?

THE SKEELS STUDIES

In the early twentieth century, when safeguards for research involving children were not widely adopted, a psychologist named Harold Skeels did a fascinating study of the power of the family unit.[5]

Skeels, who ran an orphanage, worked with twenty-five children, up to the age of two years old, who had been illegitimate and given up for adoption, or who had been abandoned or abused by their parents and taken away. One group, let's call them Group A, consisted of thirteen children, who were determined by staff to be "mentally retarded," meaning that they were of below-average intelligence. A second group of twelve children, Group B, were determined to have above-average intelligence.

Skeels made the "mentally retarded children" of Group A eligible to be adopted by families, and these children were quickly placed. In their new families, the children from Group A were able to establish positive rapports with "mother- and father-surrogates" and siblings in a home setting. On the other hand, the children in Group B, the smarter children, were not put up for adoption but remained in the "non-stimulating environment" of the orphanage.[6]

Skeels tested the children from the two groups two years later and found dramatic shifts in intelligence. During the two-year period, the "mentally retarded" children of Group A who had been adopted had increased their intelligence by an average of 28 points, from below average to above average, while the IQs of the initially more intelligent children, who had not been adopted, declined by an average of 26 points, from above average to below average.

The 54-point transformation (Group A up by 28 and Group B down by 26) became apparent after only two years![7] For experts in psychometrics, an increase or decrease of only a few points on an intelligence test could be considered significant; 54 points is absolutely astonishing.

Meeting with the children after they had become adults more than twenty years later, Skeels found that 100 percent of the children who had been originally diagnosed as being "mentally retarded" from Group A (those who were adopted), turned out to be well-adjusted, happy adults. Of the group of "initially smarter children" from Group B (those who had not been adopted), only one of the twelve could be considered well-adjusted or happy.[8]

As adults, ten of the children in Group B had wound up in institutions designated for the mentally ill. One of the children in Group B died. All the children in Group B ended up struggling financially, psychologically, and socially as adults.[9] A summary of Skeels's results can be found in figure 1.1.[10]

A major finding of the Skeels studies, corroborated by hundreds of subsequent adoption studies,[11] is that the quality of the relationship with a caregiver is paramount. The caregiver does not have to be related by blood and does not have to possess any particular characteristic other than a willingness to spend the time and effort required to demonstrate care.[12]

Lesson one from the Skeels studies: Growing up in a loving home greatly improves the probability that a child will be smart, healthy, and well-adjusted.

Lesson two: Loneliness makes you crazy.

More recent research has confirmed Skeels's initial conclusions about the devastating effects of neglect on a child's development, but with a twist.[13] With newly available technologies, neuroscientists have found that a lack of care actually damages the physical structure of a child's brain.[14] Perhaps surprisingly, neuroscientists have found that a caring environment, but one that lacks stimulation can also hinder brain development.[15]

The ideal home environment should be not only secure but also pleasant and intellectually interesting.[16] While safety is good, "low levels of stimulation . . . result in negative psychological effects upon children's development."[17] An active, fun, supportive home environment is necessary to foster healthy brains and happy children.[18]

Make Home Not Only Loving and Safe But Also Fun and Interesting

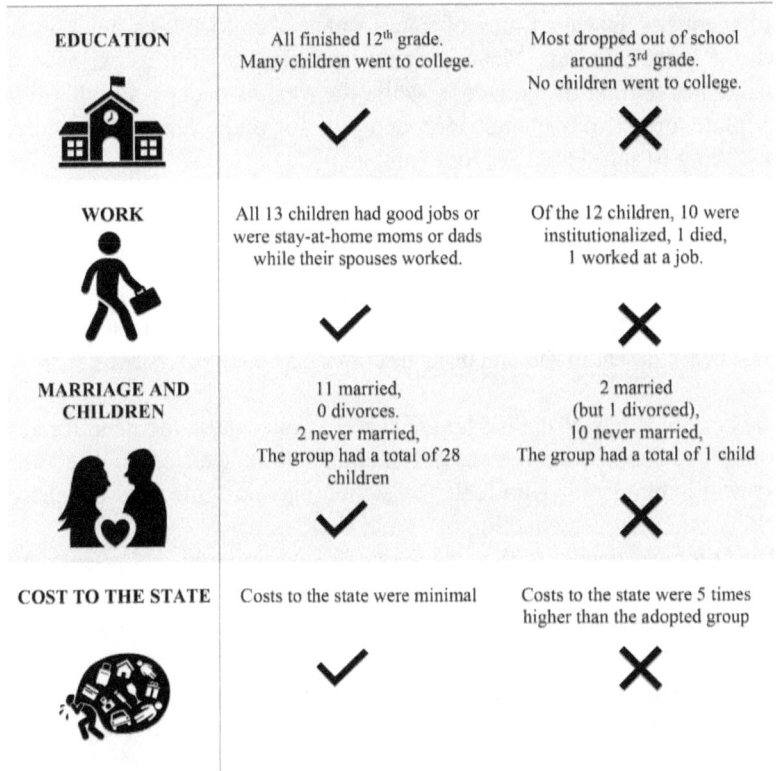

Figure 1.1 The Effects of Adoption into Caring Families, Twenty-Plus Years After Adoption (Skeels).

This is a critical point that many well-intentioned parents fail to heed, so it is worth restating. The ideal home environment should be not only safe and nurturing[19] but also pleasant and intellectually interesting.[20]

THE FAMOUS HIERARCHY OF HUMAN NEEDS

As with any well-known theory, the hierarchy of needs developed by Abraham Maslow has its proponents and detractors,[21] but the original conception of needs having five levels—physiological, safety, belonging, esteem, self-actualization—is brilliant—and a useful framework for parenting.[22] The hierarchy of needs originally was conceived as a ladder. Maslow never created a pyramid, and he did not like how representations of the hierarchy of needs as a pyramid implied that basic needs were somehow distinctive "stages."[23]

Some children may try to meet several different kinds of needs simultaneously. During times of catastrophe, a child might quickly move down the ladder, not up. Metaphorically speaking, a child might have their feet on a lower rung of the ladder, while their hands occupy a higher rung.[24] They may suffer from malnutrition and fear for their safety while they are also seeking to self-actualize, for example.

About the hierarchy of needs, Maslow writes:

> Reversals of the average order of the hierarchy are sometimes observed. Also, it has been observed that an individual may permanently lose the higher wants in the hierarchy under special conditions. There are . . . multiple motivations for usual behavior, but in addition many determinants other than motives.[25]

At the bottom rungs of the ladder are survival and safety, the need for access to sufficient food, water, rest, and shelter.[26] It is well established that a child who is hungry or who feels threatened may struggle to concentrate on anything other than satisfaction of unmet basic needs.[27]

Psychological needs, such as a sense of belonging and self-esteem, affect how children see the world and how they come to view their own place in it.[28] Children whose basic needs have not been met and who have failed to form healthy attachments early in life tend to (1) be mistrustful, (2) have low self-esteem, and (3) hold a pessimistic worldview.[29] On the other hand, children whose basic needs have been met and who have developed healthy attachments typically tend to (1) be trusting, (2) have healthy self-esteem, and (3) hold optimistic worldviews.[30]

STORY

A five-year-old boy named Felix had a mother and father who always fought. The dad was a sometimes employed, volatile alcoholic who would disappear for weeks at a time. One day, the child's mother packed up a suitcase, put him in the car, and they drove to California. The mother knew no one in the state, had no money, and took a job at the first place that offered one—a twenty-four-hour restaurant located close to the beach.

Felix and his mom lived in their car in the parking lot behind the restaurant for about a year. Felix slept in the car while his mother worked the night shift as a waitress. During her breaks, she would walk out to the car to check on her son. Felix used the public toilet and the open shower at the beach as his bathroom.

Today, Felix does not recall the time with anxiety or horror; it was just life as he knew it. From the perspective of a five-year-old boy, living in the car with his mom seemed like a pretty good life, certainly better than living in a house where his crazy dad might show up and start shoving him and his mom around.

Home can be anywhere—a shack, a mansion, a tent, a car—as long as it is a place where a child can feel cared for, a place that is interesting, a place where the child will never be turned away.

Strategy 2

Pay Attention

A widely available instrument that evaluates a home in terms of its desirability for children is suitably called the HOME, or Home Observation for Measurement of the Environment.[1] The HOME assesses "within a naturalistic context, the quality and quantity of stimulation and support available to a child."[2] HOME ratings have been established to indicate the suitability of environments for children of all ages, from newborns to adolescents. The first two criteria on the HOME assessment are responsivity and acceptance.

Responsivity simply means paying attention. When a child says, "I don't want to go to school. I hate school," a reply such as "What about school do you dislike? You have so many friends there" followed by a few minutes of intensive listening would be considered *responsive*. Saying "Shut up and eat your breakfast!" would be considered *unresponsive*.

Acceptance means giving the child sufficient leeway to learn through trial and error. An old Nike commercial from the 1990s featured Michael Jordan, who said in a voiceover:

> I've missed more than 9,000 shots in my career/ I've lost almost 300 games/ 26 times I've been trusted to take the game winning shot/ and missed./ I've failed over, and over and over again in my life./ And that is why/ I succeed.[3]

Trial and error is a fundamental way that children learn. As a parent, an overpowering urge is to want to save your child from failure and suffering. But, intervening to prevent mistakes can have detrimental effects on a child's self-confidence and sense of autonomy.[4] Care is important, but it is also important to give children enough room to succeed or fail on their own terms.

A responsive comment to a child crying would involve saying something like, "What has made you sad?" or "I get sad sometimes, too." An unresponsive response would be to say, "Stop with the tears, you crybaby," or "You cry over the stupidest things."

Strong parental responsivity and acceptance are highly correlated with healthy early cognitive development.[5] On the other hand, a lack of responsivity and acceptance may lead to "prominent deficits" and "poorer child outcome in all functioning areas."[6] Responsivity as a parent never ends. In fact, a "parent's responsivity to the child, especially in the form of verbal communications" actually increases in importance as the child grows older.[7]

Just spending time with children—walking, playing, listening, talking—is fundamental.[8] The old saying that children should be seen and not heard is actually detrimental to a child's proper brain development. In fact, parental verbal interactions have been shown to exert a tremendous influence on a child's development.[9]

In one famous study, interactions between parents and children in many different kinds of households were recorded and analyzed over a period of several years.[10] The researchers found that parents who were "professionals," those with middle or high incomes, spoke an average of 487 utterances per hour with their children. When professional parents communicated with their children, the ratio of positive to negative comments was 6:1, or 6 positive comments for every negative comment.

In welfare homes, parents averaged 178 utterances per hour with a ratio of positive to negative comments of 1:2, or one positive comment for every two negative comments. Not only did professional parents talk to their children

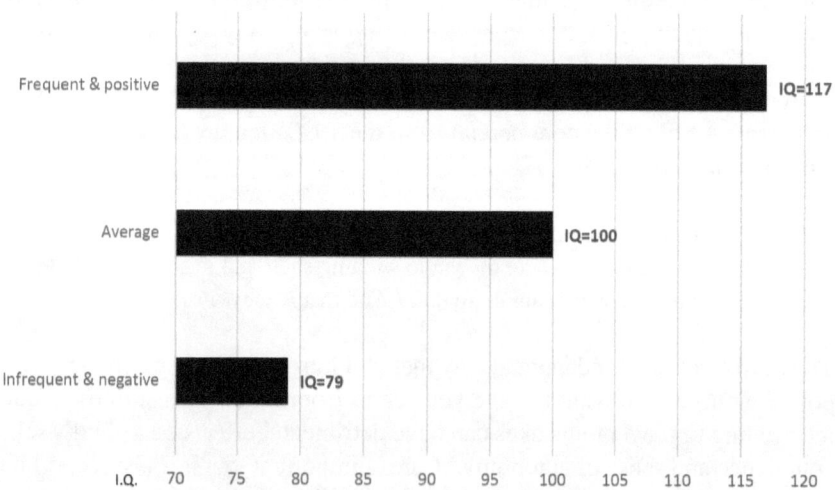

Figure 2.1 Average IQ of Children at Age Three After Positive and Frequent Verbal Interactions with Parents versus Average IQ of Children at Age Three After Negative and Infrequent Verbal Interactions with Parents.

more frequently, but they were also much more encouraging in their verbal interactions.[11] These remarkable differences were observed in only one hour.

By age three, the average IQ of the children who had professional parents zoomed to 117 while the average IQ of the children of welfare parents settled to around 79.[12]

This is the way in which "gaps" in achievement and intelligence develop over time, as illustrated in figure 2.1.[13]

After three years, the children of professional parents cumulatively had heard thirty million more words than children of welfare parents.[14] The stark differences in the home environment make it easy to understand how large differences in IQ in young children can develop over time.[15] Frequent engagement through language and a positive rapport with parents are foundational for the development of intelligence.[16]

Sometimes, parents can be seen chatting away with their children while sitting in a car at a stoplight or while they are pushing a cart around the grocery store. While some people might be irritated by such conversations, they are essential, brain-building moments for children. Conversely, scant engagement through language or negative verbal interactions with parents is harmful.[17]

Placing a screen in front of a child in a car while the parent drives, for example, might offer a brief interlude of peace and quiet, but such a practice does not benefit the child because it shuts out language. For a healthy brain, a child needs human interaction, conversation, and interesting experiences.

This line of research also offers implications for parents who do lots of talking on the phone to friends or business associates. Parents who choose to talk on the phone rather than converse in person with their own children are losing a great opportunity to foster their children's brain development.[18]

STORY

When former president Theodore Roosevelt was a child, he was fascinated by the great outdoors and used to drag home a variety of "specimens," dead birds, bugs, mice, and assorted other critters.[19] Throughout his childhood, Teddy had been feeble and sickly, continually plagued by asthma.

It would have been easy for his parents to suggest that Teddy curtail his exuberant outdoor activities and instead focus on less strenuous tasks that did not always leave him filthy, foul-smelling, and exhausted at the end of the day. But, his parents accepted Teddy as he was, despite knowing that the hope that he "not get dirty" would be seldom realized.

Roosevelt, the man, eventually went on to become police commissioner of New York City, assistant secretary of the U.S. Navy, governor, vice president, and president of the United States for two terms.[20] In addition, Roosevelt was "adept in the modern sciences . . . a statesman who was extraordinarily well versed in geography—historical, political, physical, and commercial—who was strongly interested in botany, zoology, philology, modern history, sociology."[21]

Unquestionably, Roosevelt's parental support during his early years contributed to his prodigious success as a politician, scientist, and writer. Over the course of his life, he authored thirty-five books on topics ranging from history to zoology.

Strategy 3

Have Plenty of Print Materials and Toys on Hand

In addition to conversations with adults, another important way that children learn new words is through inferring word meanings in context while reading.[1] Reading builds strong brains and helps increase vocabularies, a gift that accompanies children throughout their lives.[2] Indeed, larger vocabularies enable the possibility for understanding more written material, thereby continually increasing the child's range of expression and linguistic power.[3]

In general, the more a child reads, the larger a child's vocabulary becomes.[4] The "relationship between vocabulary and general intelligence is one of the most robust findings in the history of intelligence-testing."[5] Voracious readers continually extend their knowledge of words and sentences every time they read a new book, article, or story.

On the other hand, students typically do not encounter unfamiliar words while watching image-based media, such as films, television shows, or streamed video.[6] Scripts for image-based media tend to feature simple words and are usually written at a third-grade reading level or lower.[7]

How much do children read today? The Organization of Economic Co-operation and Development (OECD) compiles information about students, their families, and schools throughout the world, including student test scores on the Program for International Student Achievement (PISA), an assessment that measures the ability of fifteen-year-olds to use "knowledge and skills to meet real-life challenges."[8] The massive OECD databases contain detailed information on homes, parents, schools, and students in eighty countries, including the United States.[9]

A host of statistical tests were run on the OECD databases to determine which characteristics in the home environment correlated most strongly with high student achievement. The ensuing findings were quite startling, depicted in figure 3.1.[10]

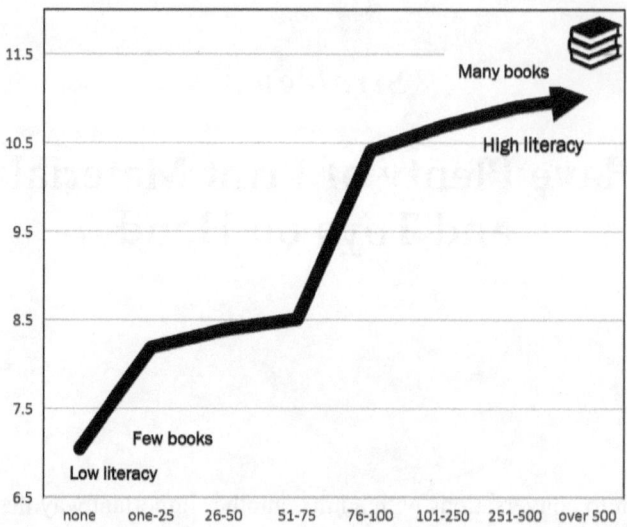

Figure 3.1 Literacy Scores and Number of Books at Home.

Having more books in the home had a stronger correlation to student achievement than any other single factor, including family income and parents' level of education.[11] The factor most strongly associated with high scores on all three tests—reading, problem-solving, and mathematics—was the number of books at home. Across categories of race, gender, and nationality, the more books in the home, the higher a student's level of achievement.[12] Apparently, what author Roald Dahl wrote is true: "If you are going to get anywhere in life you have to read a lot of books."[13]

The parts of the brain associated with reading also control "thinking, learning, speech, emotions and planned muscle movements."[14] Reading has been shown to activate different regions of the brain, "including bilateral interior frontal, superior temporal, middle temporal, middle frontal, superior frontal, and postcentral gyri, as well as bilateral occipital cortex, inferior parietal lobules, thalami, and insulae."[15] In other words, many parts of the brain are activated when a child reads.

Much like lifting weights adds muscle to the body, neuroscientists have found that time spent reading makes parts of the brain physically larger.[16] Conversely, these same regions of the brain may shrink or wither when children do not read.[17]

A stimulating home environment includes access to not only abundant print resources but also plenty of play materials and toys.[18] The mention of the word "toys" might bring to mind branded, commercial products, such as

Barbie, Disney-themed plush toys, or Star Wars action figures. However, toys could just as well be dead bugs, as in Theodore Roosevelt's case (see Strategy 2), or a bunch of empty cardboard boxes, as described in the story at the end of this chapter.

Supplying the home with play materials and toys does not necessitate spending gobs of money. The goal is to have a lively and interesting environment, not a collection of the latest offerings from corporate toy manufacturers. A seminal research study on play materials found that "the availability of toys and learning materials, the parent's involvement and encouragement of the child, and the variety of experiences to which the child is exposed" are associated with higher intellect beginning at age two.[19] In contrast, "an inadequate or insufficient environmental stimulation is a major contributing factor of the developmental lag in . . . brain maturation."[20]

The mathematical equation for a healthy brain is as follows:

$$\frac{\begin{array}{c}\text{A safe and interesting home +}\\ \text{a parent's encouragement +}\\ \text{a home full of toys +}\\ \text{a home full of books}\end{array}}{\text{Healthy brain}}$$

A responsive school can help counteract the negative effects of a home environment that might score poorly on the HOME assessment.[21] However, children who live in dysfunctional homes and attend ineffective, uncaring schools face a "double disadvantage" with regard to brain development.[22] In contrast, a "double advantage," meaning a safe, stimulating home environment and a caring, effective school, is the preferred scenario.

STORY

A Child Development Center for children, aged three to four, located on the campus of a prestigious university, was widely known as the absolute best place within hundred miles for child care for young children and it received a grant to build "the world's greatest playground" on the campus.

On the day that the world's greatest playground was to debut, hundreds of parents and their children showed up for the ribbon-cutting ceremony. However, after the ribbon was cut and the speeches were made, very few children were playing on the new, expensive playground. Where did they go? They were playing in the grassy area next to the playground, among the mountain of discarded cardboard boxes that were used to transport the playground equipment.

Play is essential to a young child's healthy development and is positively associated with increased creativity, cooperation, openness, and intelligence.[23] "Play is by its very nature educational. And it should be pleasurable. When the fun goes out of play, most often so does the learning."[24]

Strategy 4

Limit Screen Time

The American Psychological Association defines screen time as "any interaction with a screen, including watching television/content, internet, social media and app use, gaming . . . on any platform (phones, tablets, computers, television)."[1] These days, screens—watches, phones, tablets, computers, televisions, video game consoles—are everywhere.[2]

We carry screens around in our pockets, spend long days staring at them in our jobs, seek them out for entertainment, use them to communicate, and consult them for updates on the condition of the world.[3] A phone is the first thing most Americans reach for in the morning and the last thing they touch before going to sleep at night.[4]

Undeniably, screens are powerful and can offer access to infinite amounts of information, but their misuse can wreak substantial harm. The American Academy of Pediatrics is unequivocal with regard to screen time for young children, recommending children under the age of two have zero, that is, absolutely no exposure to screens at all, save possibly the occasional video chat with family. Yet, in the United States today, most two-year-olds not only spend hours with screens, but they also have their own phones.[5] Two-year-olds.[6]

Researchers in education and the neurosciences have found four pernicious effects of too much screen time for children:[7]

1. Damaged cognitive functioning[8]
2. Poor health and fitness[9]
3. Poor attention and problem behavior[10]
4. Impaired or deficient sleep[11]

None of these four negative effects on children is good news. Yet, despite the repeated warnings about potentially detrimental effects of excessive screen time, many parents continue to offer unrestricted, unsupervised access to screens.[12] In fact, a recent survey found that 90 percent of parents actively encouraged their young children to view online videos.[13]

These trends are alarming, particularly when taken in the context of other findings—that parents acknowledge that "inappropriate" online Internet videos abound—and that their children already "spend too much time with screens."[14] Some screen time is not bad, of course, but screens have crowded out books and reading.[15] It is not as if there is nothing to read, as more than 300,000 new books typically get published in the United States every year.[16] Teens spend even more time with screens than young children, logging, on average, eight hours of screen time every day.[17]

A ratio of 1:1, an hour of reading for every hour spent with screens, might be acceptable, but the ratio of screen time to reading time for children is nowhere close to 1:1. For adolescents, the ratio is 26:1, meaning that for every hour spent reading, teens spend twenty-six hours watching videos and playing video games.[18] In case you are wondering, the researchers who created the media-use survey classified reading on digital devices in the category of reading, not screen time.[19]

Superb, inventive educational software is available, but it takes technological savvy and diligence to ensure that children stay focused on the intellectual challenges of the task at hand. It takes less than a second to click away from a free e-book on Gutenberg.org to the latest viral video on TikTok.

If the recommendations of the American Academy of Pediatrics concerning the harmful effects of too much screen time are not convincing enough, consider that children who were heavy users of screens scored more than two grade levels lower than light users of screens on recent tests of reading and mathematics.[20]

In summary, the data is unequivocal regarding children and screens. No screen time is recommended for children under two; a maximum of an hour per day for children aged two to five; two hours a day max for everyone else. Instead of staring at screens, children might actually prefer reading, conversation with family, outdoor activities, or exploring new places.

STORY

In a recent interview about technology, virtual reality pioneer Jaron Lanier observed that "the more a parent is involved in the technology industry, the more cautious they seem to be about their kids' interactions with it. A lot of parents in Silicon Valley purposefully seek out anti-tech environments for their kids."[21] Indeed, while the Internet can provide timely, useful information, it can also be a time-sucking, addictive, black hole.[22]

Bill and Melinda Gates (Microsoft), Steve and Laurene Jobs (Apple), and Sundar and Anjali Pichai (Google) all severely restricted access to technology when their children were young.[23] It is instructive to look at the practices of billionaire parents, who made their fortunes in technology, when formulating policies on screen time for your own children. If mandating limits on screen time was good enough for the children of tech billionaires, perhaps . . .

Strategy 5

Get Moving and Get Outside

No one ever forgets how to ride a bicycle because physical movement has a way of lodging itself into long-term memory.[1] An eight-year-old boy, for example, might have been forced to participate in a music class where he learned how to square dance. Although he might have had little occasion to utilize his square-dancing abilities since age eight, he likely would still remember how to *dosado*, *promenade*, and *twirl*.

He would remember how to square dance, not because he has consistently completed worksheets on square dancing for homework over the past twenty years and not because he has taken a battery of multiple-choice tests on square dancing, but because movement is a completely natural, enduring, often effortless way to learn.

Jean Piaget called the initial phase of child development *the sensorimotor stage* because he discovered that a young child's intellectual maturation was largely dependent upon movement and touch.[2] A child's earliest expressions of mind are communicated through unintelligible vocalizations and physical gestures.

Since Piaget's time, researchers have discovered that limited interactions with the physical world can lead to blunted brain development and a host of other problems.[3] Recent studies have even found that many learning disabilities are not caused by physical defects of the brain, but are due to a child's insufficient interplay with the physical world in the early years of life.[4]

Movement is necessary for proper physical and mental development. However, as children get older, schools typically provide less opportunity for movement and fewer chances to play.[5] It is estimated that "play time" for the average school-age child in the United States has been cut in half over the past twenty years.[6] In most schools, outside recess during school hours stops at fifth or sixth grade.[7]

Although physical education classes might at least get kids out-of-doors, fitness classes are no longer required in most schools.[8] Despite the conspicuous absence of exercise in the official K–12 curriculum, research is clear that children who are physically active perform much better in school than children who are not physically active.[9]

Regretfully, the school day seems to be designed to encourage docility and submission, requiring children to sit quietly and motionlessly for seven to eight hours per day with only short, five-minute breaks in between.[10] For most children, school translates into over 1,000 hours of sitting quietly every year.[11]

A recent article in the *Journal of the American Medical Association* notes that so much sitting has been "associated with increased risk of obesity, cardiovascular disease, cancer, diabetes, and overall mortality."[12] Although the data concerning the benefits of physical movement are indisputable, children still spend most of their time—90 percent of their lives—inside buildings, engaged in sedentary tasks.[13]

The biological systems of most children burn with excess energy, their emotions can fluctuate minute-by-minute, and their brains relentlessly seek the manna of new experiences, so sitting still for hours on end can be difficult, to say the least.[14] In response to the trend of increased "butt-in-seat" time in schools, a countermovement sponsored by ecology groups and naturalists was launched, called *No Child Left Inside*.[15] The premise of *No Child Left Inside* was that children who did not venture into the outdoors could develop symptoms of *Nature Deficit Disorder*, a condition that might lead to a host of problems, including hyperactivity, an inability to focus, higher levels of anxiety, and irrational thinking.[16]

While some people might roll their eyes about the dangers of spending too much time indoors, hundreds of studies substantiate the mental, emotional, and physical benefits of spending time outside, in natural environments.[17]

Children diagnosed with Attention Deficit Disorder or Attention Deficit Hyperactivity Disorder, in particular, seem to reap significant benefits from spending time in nature.[18] Even walks of only twenty minutes in a natural environment have been shown to help restore attention spans and reduce off-task behaviors in hyperactive children.[19]

Perhaps the uncontrollable variables of life outdoors, such as insects, animals, geography, and weather force the mind to anticipate contingent and unpredictable events.[20] Being active in natural settings promotes "development of intrapersonal and interpersonal skills, exposes children to a degree of physical and psychological risk that supports their sense of autonomy, competence and relatedness and contributes to the development of risk management."[21] Explorations in the great outdoors have been found to improve a child's creative and analytic thinking.[22]

Research findings have consistently shown beneficial results from spending time in nature.

1. *Being outdoors can help improve a child's attitude and vitality.*
   "More time that children spend in natural environments has a positive effect on dispositions and level of energy."[23]
2. *Being outdoors can spur creativity.*
   "Maximal improvements in creative thinking associated with a media-free, outdoor environment, may occur after a relatively short exposure time."[24]
3. *Being outdoors can promote fitness.*
   "Children who spend time outdoors are more likely to be physically active, have a healthy weight, spend less time in sedentary activities, have better motor skills."[25]
4. *Being outdoors can improve psychological well-being.*
   "Access to green space was associated with improved mental well-being, overall health and cognitive development of children."[26]

When children are exposed to a variety of outdoor activities, their creative thinking, self-esteem, and sense of gratitude tend to increase when compared to children who remain indoors.[27] So, if a problem needs to get sorted out or if a child is distraught, sometimes a simple walk together to the nearest park can work wonders.

There is also something in nature that nurtures the creative spirit. The poet Nathaniel Mackey said,

> You go out and you look in the sky. We live in this act of creation that is unfathomable and overwhelming. The intricacy, beauty, fearsomeness. We push back by becoming active, becoming producers, and putting our little pieces of creativity down next to it. It's this idea, I can do something, too.[28]

STORY

The writer Ralph Waldo Emerson had four children with his wife Lidian. Whenever one of his children became upset, he would ask them to go outside and study a cloud formation, a tree, or a flower and these interactions with nature seemed to calm their anger or sadness.[29] Indeed, Emerson resolutely believed in the power of nature to foster hope and transcend disappointment. In an essay Emerson entitled *Nature*, he wrote:

> Nature is made to conspire with spirit to emancipate us. Certain mechanical changes, a small alteration in our local position apprizes us of a dualism. We are strangely affected by seeing the shore from a moving ship, from a balloon, or through the tints of an unusual sky. The least change in our point of view gives the whole world a pictorial air.[30]

Emerson had many friends and admirers, among them Nathaniel Hawthorne, Walt Whitman, Louisa May Alcott, Margaret Fuller, Horace Mann, John Muir, John Brown (the abolitionist), Herman Melville, William Wordsworth, Henry James, Henry David Thoreau, and Elizabeth Peabody.[31] Friends understood that when they visited Emerson, they would not be spending much time sitting on a couch by the fire. Emerson liked to walk as he talked. He wrote, "In the woods . . . a man casts off his years, as the snake his slough and at what period so ever of life is always a child. In the woods is perpetual youth."[32]

Strategy 6

Engage with the Arts

As cardboard boxes and dead bugs can serve as toys, twigs and empty bottles can serve as objects for a visual arts project or as musical instruments for the spontaneous creation of a song. The arts provide an outlet for feeling and thought and, once a project is completed, children are left with an artifact of their own creation.

The arts are one of the few areas of life in which the goal is to create something original and beautiful rather than functional or efficient.[1] "The arts" consist of music (instrumental and vocal), dance, drama, creative writing, architecture, painting, sculpture, photography, graphic design, crafts, fashion design, movies, television, radio, and sound recording.[2] Unquestionably, the arts present an attractive array of choices.

One reason to get a child involved with the arts is because these activities can be lots of fun! A second reason is that you might want to see if a child might possess artistic or musical talent. Evidence overwhelmingly suggests that a child's eventual success in the arts is contingent upon the support of a caring adult.

> The gift is never fully developed when first observed, and must be nourished through daily training ... all [successful adult artists] report having had at least one parent or teacher who cared deeply about their talent, and who worked with them daily, sitting with them as they practiced and establishing a structure of discipline.[3]

Children like to draw, but often their interest in drawing is temporary and contingent. One five-year-old I spoke with in a kindergarten class recently churned out three different drawings in about ten minutes. Each drawing had a story, which he was happy to share, but he spent more time explaining the three drawings than he spent actually creating them. Of course, ten minutes spent in drawing is still time well spent, but a focus solely on creating new art can get quickly tiresome for a young child.

Most children do not know how to approach art.[4] What makes a drawing good? Is a child capable of making a drawing that is realistic and compelling? How do children move from creating "tadpole" drawings, representations of people as large circles with sticks for arms and legs, to expressive art?[5] Should children just be "left alone" with regard to art?

As a parent, a useful way to think about the arts is to consider them in three parts, as depicted in figure 6.1.[6]

At the age of eight, Pablo Picasso used oil-based paints to create *Picador*, a painting of a scene at a bullfight.[7] Completed even before Picasso had his first art lesson, *Picador* would have been an achievement for most adult artists, let alone a child of eight. Because his father was a teacher and a painter, he had introduced Pablo to painting at a very early age.[8] Would Picasso have become an artist if his father had been a merchant who considered drawing a waste of time?[9] It seems unlikely.

The arts' uncanny power offers children a chance to express themselves unbounded by their limited experience. Until the mid-twentieth century, most scientists considered the arts to be largely irrelevant to health and well-being,[10] but in recent decades, a multitude of studies, many of them situated

Figure 6.1   Three Ways of Engaging with the Arts.

in schools and hospitals, have confirmed that the arts can have therapeutic effects on brain, body, and emotions.[11]

As a result, organizations focused on the healing effects of the arts have sprung up across the United States—the American Art Therapy Association, the American Music Therapy Association, and the American Dance Therapy Association, to name a few. These organizations have been founded upon the belief that purposeful, arts-based interventions can be used to address psychological and physical problems.[12] The areas in which the therapeutic arts have been proven effective include "maternity, neonatal and intensive care, . . . cardiovascular conditions, surgery and pain management, lung diseases, and oncology."[13]

The rise of the therapeutic arts has coincided with a trend in the medical sciences to view children more holistically so that a child is "perceived as a human being whose needs are discussed on three equally important dimensions: biological, social and psychological."[14] Perhaps the most startling finding about the arts is that they can actually alter a child's biological responses.[15] Scientific studies have demonstrated that the arts can have a potentially powerful influence on the mind and body. Recent studies of participation in the arts have found five particularly significant benefits.

1. *The arts can have a soothing effect.*
   "Art making resulted in statistically significant lowering of cortisol levels."[16] [High cortisol levels are associated with high stress]
2. *The arts can promote healing.*
   "The use of art . . . reduced hospital stays, with studies showing earlier discharges among patients taking part in visual and performing arts interventions."[17]
3. *The arts can reduce the incidence of depression.*
   "Art therapy . . . significantly improved cancer-related anxiety and depression and reduced the prevalence of severe anxiety and depression during cancer treatment."[18]
4. *The arts can help regulate executive functions.*
   The arts program is associated with an increase in self-regulation and "an increase in anger control."[19]
5. *The arts can promote empathy.*
   "Theater, drama and visual arts . . . promote empathy."[20]

The arts can help children communicate about everyday life, about "experiences that are too difficult to put into words," and about experiences for which they lack the vocabulary to describe.[21] Indeed, a common tactic for discerning the thoughts and feelings of traumatized children is to encourage them to express themselves through the arts.[22]

In addition to their therapeutic value, the arts are enjoyable and easy to integrate at home and school. A piece of chalk and a bit of pavement, a stick and a bottle, the humming of a musical tune—the arts can be inexpensive and spontaneous, yet also thoroughly satisfying.

As the theologian and writer Thomas Merton wrote in his book *No Man is an Island*, "Art enables us to find ourselves and lose ourselves at the same time."[23]

STORY

After World War II, Margaret Naumburg encountered many children who had been tortured, beaten, starved, and/or left in isolation for extended periods of time by the Nazis.[24] Most of these children had been severely traumatized and had a wide range of psychological disorders.[25] Naumburg managed to "get inside" the hearts and minds of these traumatized children to help them recover through the arts.[26]

Children who had not been responsive to any other intervention came alive when Naumburg brought out the paints and paper.[27] According to Naumburg, when traumatized children started drawing, "interior images of the unconscious" got transferred into pictures which served "as a substitute for words or as a stimulus which leads to an increase of verbalization."[28]

Art can be equally powerful when used with non-traumatized children, "not only because it serves another language but also because of its inherent ability to help people of all ages explore emotions and beliefs, reduce stress, resolve problems and conflicts, and enhance their sense of well-being."[29]

Strategy 7

Help Your Child Choose a Musical Instrument

A depressed, listless, ten-year-old boy named Mark was diagnosed with a brain tumor and given only a few months to live.[1] Despite battling nausea, dizziness, and a rapidly deteriorating condition, a musical therapist worked with Mark to learn how to play the drums, which he had never previously attempted. When learning to play the drums, the therapist reported that "the sheer aliveness and joy of the music surprises both of us, and Mark seems to gain physical energy as he plays."[2]

Concerning the age when musical training should begin, Hungarian composer Zoltán Kodály suggested a time "nine months before the birth of the mother."[3] In other words, a child should engage with music as soon as possible. Researchers have found that first graders taught music through singing, dancing, clapping, and hand signals showed significantly higher reading scores when compared to comparable groups of first graders who had no musical training.

In most of the published studies concerning the effects of musical training on academic skills, children who receive at least some musical training perform better than children who receive no musical training. The academic gains associated with music seem to endure for years.[4]

Also, consider that each branch of the U.S. military—Air Force, Army, Coast Guard, Marines, and Navy—supports their own musical groups. Providing music for soldiers costs the government more than a half billion dollars per year.[5] Although some critics have lambasted the armed services for spending so much money on music, the costs seem meager in relation to music's benefits, and many studies have substantiated the value of music to soldiers.[6]

A group of researchers from the University of South Florida worked with children under the age of eighteen who had been convicted of felony crimes.

In interactions with these juvenile felons, it was learned that most were extremely poor readers, typically more than two grades behind their peers. Researchers tried several methods to improve the reading comprehension of these children and, after many years of trial and error, finally found something that worked.

The winning formula involved a computer game called "Singing Coach" that asked players to learn the lyrics of popular songs and to sing along while the program discerned the extent to which each player enunciated the words properly and sang on key.[7] The player who sang the lyrics correctly and sang in tune most often won the game.

These incarcerated juveniles quickly became engaged with "Singing Coach" and, in order to perform well at the game, they had to learn to sight-read hundreds of words and to pronounce them clearly. As a result, their sight vocabulary improved, and they became better readers. Some students advanced as much as three grade levels in reading comprehension in only a matter of months.[8]

Volumes of studies support the positive effects of music, including the following five benefits.[9]

1. *Music can improve memory.*

    Music "has been repeatedly shown to stimulate cortical areas of the brain associated with memory, motor function and auditory and visual circuits."[10]

2. *Music can benefit language development.*

    "Children who completed 2 years of music training had a stronger neurophysiological distinction of stop consonants, a neural mechanism linked to reading and language skills."[11]

3. *Music from mothers can dramatically improve their children's health.*

    "A mother singing lullabies can have beneficial effects on [a child's] weight gain, oxygen saturation improvements, feeding and crying."[12]

4. *Music can strengthen the immune system.*

    "Music can calm neural activity in the brain, which may lead to reductions in anxiety, and that it may help to restore effective functioning in the immune system partly via the actions of the amygdala and hypothalamus."[13]

5. *Music is inexpensive and easy to access.*

    Music "is classified as a non-pharmacological and independent nursing intervention. It is a non-invasive, well tolerated, and cheap intervention."[14]

Participation in band, choir, or orchestra at school can be enjoyable and helps establish a peer group of friends. So, participation in music programs at school can be beneficial, but it is also true that the family's influence is typically much greater than a school's in fostering musical ability.[15] Musically gifted children "often make their best, most inventive work out of school."[16]

There are millions of inspiring quotes about the power of music, but this one from Plato from *The Republic* is especially compelling:

> Musical training is a more potent instrument than any other, because rhythm and harmony find their way into the inward places of the soul, on which they mightily fasten, imparting grace, and making the soul of him who is rightly educated graceful, or of him who is ill-educated ungraceful.[17]

Encouraging children to select a musical instrument is more than suggesting that they take up a hobby. You want "rhythm and harmony" to "find their way into the inward places of the soul" so they can experience the incomparable sense of grace that music can deliver.

STORY

A child is typically fascinated with how a pianist can produce beautiful sounds from a heavy, big, wooden box. After listening to music, a child might climb up on the piano bench, move her fingers across the piano keys, and imagine the kind of music she might make.

From a very early age, the piano can provide an outlet for expression, a vehicle for exploring emotions and thoughts, many of which a child may not even know she has—until she begins to play. When a pianist no longer has access to a piano, an emptiness can linger in the heart and mind until hands find their way, once again, to the keys.[18]

A child who attends an orchestra or band demonstration at an elementary school may fall in love with a variety of instruments. "The real power of music lies in the fact that it can be true to the life of feeling in a way that language cannot."[19]

For a child, any musical instrument, including the piano, violin, or trumpet (three popular instruments) might be considered. Remember that the harmonica, xylophone, and voice count as musical instruments, too. Also, for some children, no musical instrument satisfies quite like the drums.[20] The best scenario is to let the child have the final decision with regard to musical instruments, even if the one chosen is not your favorite.

Strategy 8

Seek Out Diverse Experiences

"The tendency of people to seek out those they perceive to be most like themselves" is known as *homophily*.[1] Homophily becomes quickly evident at large gatherings involving different kinds of people. At gatherings where employees from across the United States come to meet, for example, people from the same region will tend to congregate. At faculty meetings in schools, teachers with expertise in the same areas will inevitably sit together. In the hundreds of times that I have given talks in schools, all the school's coaches have clustered together, without fail.

The impulse toward homophily is strong, natural, and completely understandable. We like to associate with people with whom we share interests—a job, a hobby, or an affiliation.[2] Homophily explains the popularity of fraternities, sororities, alumni associations, and organizations such as Rotary, Shriner's, and Veterans of Foreign Wars.[3]

The downside of homophily is that spending time with others who share your interests can limit your own perspectives, eliminate possibilities for novel experiences, and reduce the likelihood of finding new friends. Someone susceptible to homophily can become territorial and distrustful of anyone outside of the group to which he/she belongs.[4]

Because social groups tend to be formed around like-mindedness on specific issues—Black Lives Matter or Back the Blue—any opinion other than the one held to be legitimate within the social circle is rarely even acknowledged.[5] As a result, sometimes a story spreads within groups, even after it has been proven to be blatantly false.[6]

Examples include the persistent belief among some people that former president Barack Obama is not a U.S. citizen, despite confirmation of the authenticity of his birth certificate and the evidence of hospital records,[7] or that humans have not really walked on the moon, despite the overwhelming evidence of moon expeditions completed by astronauts from different countries around the world.[8]

As a parent, it is easy to succumb to homophily. That is, it is easy to fall into a pattern where you and your child interact only with others who look, behave, and think just as you do.

The opposite of homophily is heterophily or the "tendency for individuals who differ from one another in some way to make social connections."[9] In general, individuals who tend toward heterophily are more extroverted, self-confident in new environments, and attracted to innovation while individuals who tend toward homophily are more introverted, uncomfortable in new environments, and resistant to change.[10] Characteristics of homophily and heterophily are depicted in figure 8.1.

Seeking out diverse experiences takes concerted, purposeful effort unless your social circle already happens to include families with different ethnicities, cultures, or incomes.

The international consulting firm McKinsey & Company recently completed a series of reports on diversity, and found that businesses that recruited and kept a multicultural workforce tended to have greater profitability, higher employee satisfaction, and higher productivity than businesses that employed a monocultural workforce.[11] In light of rapid changes in technology and burgeoning globalized trade, the World Economic Forum recommends that

	HETEROPHILY	HOMOPHILY
DISPOSITION TOWARDS OTHERS	Extroverted	Introverted
RESPONSE TO NEW ENVIRONMENTS	Self-confident	Uncomfortable
REACTION TO CHANGE	Innovate	Resist change

Figure 8.1 Characteristics of Heterophily and Homophily.

new workers possess strong "critical thinking and analysis" abilities, as well as self-management skills, such as "active learning, resilience, stress tolerance, and flexibility."[12]

Of course, homophily and heterophily are only concepts and most children display a mixture of both tendencies, depending upon the time and place. Not every experience has to be novel, but new experiences can be invaluable for brain-building and the development of compassion.[13]

Experts contend that future workers will need to be able to process complex information and be capable of working well with people from all backgrounds.[14] Critical thinking skills can be developed and honed by purposefully seeking out diverse populations[15] and learning how to foster "intercultural exchange across different kinds of cultural groups."[16]

Understanding the "decision-making processes and belief systems of other people"[17] is considered a foundational skill for the future.[18] Writer Yuval Harari suggests that schools adopt the teaching of "'the four Cs'—critical thinking, communication, collaboration and creativity."[19]

Sometimes children seem incapable of seeing themselves as someone else might see them.[20] To be sure, any sort of self-reflection is difficult for the very young.[21] One great advantage of travel is that it can help build an awareness of different ways of being at almost any age, even among children who are not naturally self-reflective.[22] In this way, travel is good for the mind, helping foster "self-identity, skill development, and social relations."[23] Indeed, travel to an unfamiliar destination can provide memorable learning experiences that can remain lodged in the brain indefinitely.[24]

Certainly, few experiences are more humbling than attempting to navigate in an unfamiliar country where you do not speak the language. Travelers to foreign lands are often forced to adjust to different ways of living, what academics call "dialectically opposed modes of adaptation to the world."[25] The disequilibrium that accompanies travel forces the mind to work harder and more imaginatively,[26] opening the space for new experiences.[27]

The scholar Joseph Campbell always credited his prodigious achievements, in part, to his parents' dedication to a sustained program of travel for him and his brother.[28] Travel does not have to last months in order to have an effect; studies have shown that even short-term travel, such as a trip to a nearby beach or a local zoo, can be transformative.[29]

Mark Twain wrote that "Travel is fatal to prejudice, bigotry, and narrow-mindedness. . . . Broad, wholesome, charitable views of men and things cannot be acquired by vegetating in one little corner of the earth all one's lifetime."[30] While visiting other countries can be fun and enlightening, travel to sites in the neighborhood also can make a significant impact.[31]

Exploring nearby parks, visiting museums, touring manufacturing plants, talking with local artists, participating in charity events, listening to presentations by local librarians, conversing with park rangers—these activities cost nothing and readily satisfy the young mind's appetite for variety.

STORY

A long-time teacher in a public school in Corpus Christi, a bustling city located along the Gulf of Mexico in South Texas, once told me that she was astounded to have adolescents in her classes who had lived in Corpus their entire lives but had never been to the beach at Padre Island. Not once.

To go from the school where she taught to Padre Island required heading south and crossing one bridge—a trip of less than 10 miles. As a teacher, she always felt that students who had never been to Padre Island were the very ones who would have benefited the most from it. That is, she said that the students who had never been to the beach were also the students who seemed most anxious, stubborn, and inflexible in their thinking. They also tended to have the lowest achievement scores.

Strategy 9

Promote Resilience

The *Oxford English Dictionary* defines *resilience* as "the quality or fact of being able to recover quickly or easily from, or resist being affected by, a misfortune, shock, or illness."[1] The good news about resilience is that it can be learned.[2] An easy way for children to learn resilience is to witness their parents or peers adroitly responding to traumatic events. "Experiences with manageable forms of stress during childhood usually contribute to one's ability to deal with stress and adversity later in life."[3]

People are considered resilient when, after they fail at a task, the focus shifts to the self, not to external, uncontrollable factors. A key to becoming resilient is the willingness to improve. Consider the following four reasons a child might offer for failing to learn how to ride a bike for the first time.

1. "I am not coordinated enough."
2. "I did not try my hardest."
3. "Riding a bike is impossible."
4. "The wind was blowing too hard."

Each of these reasons fits into a simple matrix of attribution theory, shown in figure 9.1.[4] Attribution theory gets at the question of why: the reasons why a child thinks he/she has succeeded or failed.

How a child thinks about failure is consequential. A child who says that failure is due to external factors, such as the difficulty of the task ("riding a bike is impossible") or luck ("the wind was blowing too hard"), has abdicated personal responsibility for the outcome. If a child considers a task impossible, it would be foolish to spend any time or effort on trying to accomplish it. Similarly, since a child cannot possibly control the weather, fighting against

	IN THE CONTROL OF THE INDIVIDUAL	NOT IN THE CONTROL OF THE INDIVIDUAL
CHILD'S ATTRIBUTION (STABLE)	"I am not coordinated enough."	"Riding a bike is impossible."
CAUSE OF FAILURE	Ability	Task difficulty
CHILD'S ATTRIBUTION (VARIABLE)	"I did not try my hardest."	"The wind was blowing too hard."
CAUSE OF FAILURE	Motivation	Luck

Figure 9.1 A Child's Attribution for Failure to Ride a Bicycle for the First Time.

a gust of wind would be foolish. From the child's perspective, if the external world is set against them, there is no sense in putting forth any effort.

On the other hand, when a child thinks that failure is due to a lack of ability ("I am not coordinated enough"), the solution is controllable. It just means more practice is needed so that the child's bike-riding abilities can be improved.

Effort ("I did not try hard my hardest") can vary widely according to the task, but effort is under the control of the child, too. A child who wants to ride a bike will eventually exert the effort necessary to master the task. When a child attributes failure to controllable, internal phenomena, such as effort or ability, it means that they believe they, not external forces, are in charge of outcomes.

To be sure, "success is less a result of one's abilities than of one's beliefs about one's abilities and the work put forth in improving those abilities."[5]

This conclusion about the power of "one's beliefs about one's abilities" resonates with one of the most interesting research projects on learning completed in recent years. In a study of thousands of students, researchers at The University of Chicago found success in school to be reliant upon *academic behaviors* and *academic perseverance*, both of which can be internally regulated, meaning that they are under the individual's control. *Academic behaviors* were defined as "going to class, doing homework, organizing materials, and participating."[6] Indeed, a student who consistently displays these four academic behaviors is likely to have a highly successful experience in school, no matter their level of intelligence.[7]

The five traits of academic perseverance were defined as "grit, tenacity, delayed gratification, self-discipline, and self-control." In the preface to her book entitled *Grit*, Angela Duckworth wrote this about being selected as a MacArthur Genius Fellow. "A girl who is told repeatedly that she's no genius ends up winning an award for being one. The award goes to her because she has discovered that what we eventually accomplish may depend more on our passion and perseverance than on our innate talent."[8]

Whereas resilience is the ability to "bounce back," grit is considered "perseverance and passion for long-term goals."[9] In the famous marshmallow experiments, led by Walter Mischel, experimenters told young children that if they could forego eating a marshmallow (or other kind of treat) immediately, they would be rewarded with two marshmallows later.[10]

Mischel found that the children who managed to delay gratification as four-year-olds were much more successful as adults than children who did not delay gratification. Even as adolescents, those who delayed gratification

> were more academically and socially competent than their peers and more able to cope with frustration and resist temptation. . . . [They were] more verbally fluent and able to express ideas; they used and responded to reason, were attentive and able to concentrate, to plan, and to think ahead, and were competent and skillful.[11]

Of course, Mischel's experiments do not mean that a child who has difficulty with delaying self-regulation is doomed, it just means that the pathways to success might be a little more challenging.

STORY

At some point in their lives, many people become obsessed with "making a difference." They read a slew of biographies and self-help books in the hopes of discovering what they might be able to contribute to the world. The two books under the series title *How to Get a Life* were written for such people, as they focus on *how* eminent individuals made the positive contributions that they did.[12]

What is notable is that every "great life" selected for inclusion in *How to Get a Life* experienced great anguish and failed again and again over the course of their lives. However, rather than crumble or give up in response to failure, these individuals endured, bounced back from calamities, and eventually found success. In other words, circumstances did not limit what happened in their lives; they took responsibility for what happened.

About responding to misfortune, the prolific psychologist Leo Buscaglia wrote, "We can turn despair into hope, and that's magical. We can wipe away any tears and substitute smiles. . . . There are two forces at work, external an internal. We have very little control over the external forces. . . . What really matters is the internal force. How do I respond to those disasters? Over that I have complete control."[13]

A characteristic of 100 percent of the individuals who "got a life" is that they were resilient. They were able to turn obstacles into opportunities and disasters into demonstrations of character.

Part II

AT SCHOOL

Strategy 10

Choose the Best School

While the recommendation to "choose the best school" seems like common sense, many parents use other criteria to decide upon a school for their child. Typically, convenience and proximity are the strongest factors and may overwhelm all other considerations. Still, the most convenient school is not always the best school.

Of course, the optimal situation would be where the most convenient school also happened to be the best school. But, *optimal* usually does not occur by accident but takes planning and shrewd execution.

Prestige, or a school's reputation, is a factor that some parents find irresistible. Certainly, when options abound among public, private, and charter schools, using prestige as a criterion for selection can help narrow the field. If choosing between a prestigious school and one with a poor reputation in a high-crime neighborhood, the choice should be obvious.

Some private schools are incredibly expensive, but a high price is no guarantee of high quality. To find the right fit, you have to be objective about your child's abilities, interests, and your own commitment to supporting them.

Homeschooling is an increasingly popular option for parents who have the financial assets, patience, teacherly dispositions, and time to devote to thinking up lessons continually over the course of several years. About 3 percent of America's children were homeschooled in 2020 pre-COVID-19, with most parents citing "concern over the environment of local schools" as the primary reason for keeping their children at home.[1] During COVID-19, the percentage of children being homeschool escalated to 11 percent nationally but was higher than 11 percent in many states.[2]

Parents who plan to homeschool their children may want to skip the chapters about how to select a great school.

LIFE AT SCHOOL

American children spend a substantial portion of their lives in schools, about 20,000 hours spread over thirteen to fourteen years, from prekindergarten until high school graduation. Children also spend time engaged in school-related activities in the evenings and on the weekends. While time spent at home is clearly important, much research suggests that time spent in school can contribute even more to a child's intellectual and social development.[3]

An extensive research study done by faculty at Harvard found that only one year of kindergarten was "highly correlated with outcomes such as earnings, college attendance, home ownership, and retirement savings" at age twenty-seven.[4]

Smaller class sizes and higher quality teachers in the early grades, prekindergarten to third grade, have shown to not only help sharpen a child's mind but also profoundly affect attitudes and behaviors, which can lead to improved effort and a "lack of disruptive behavior" later in life.[5] Some longitudinal studies have tracked the effects of positive early education programs all the way into middle-age.[6]

Several successful early childhood interventions, such as the Milwaukee Project,[7] the Educare Initiative,[8] and the Abecedarian Program,[9] have demonstrated that the advantages of attending a good school and having a good teacher in the early years can last a lifetime.[10]

Another highly successful early school intervention was called the Perry Preschool Project. The creators of the Perry Preschool Project used common sense and human compassion as the program's basic building blocks. Their goal was simple—to encourage children to be active, independent, and articulate in oral and written language. The Perry Project hired caring teachers who helped facilitate each student's success through lots of positive, interpersonal interaction.

The original Perry study randomly selected three- and four-year-old African American children from high-poverty families to receive this "treatment." Researchers caught up with Perry Preschool Project participants when they were in their late twenties and compared their success against those who had not participated in the Perry Preschool Project.

They found that children who participated in the Perry Preschool Project (the right school in figure 10.1) had committed significantly fewer crimes, were less reliant on welfare, and had a lower incidence of childbirth outside of marriage than kids who went to the wrong school (or no school). The Perry Preschool Project kids as adults were also wealthier, were more likely to own their homes, and had higher levels of education.

Although the Perry Project involved very young children, a change to a better school can yield benefits at any point in a child's life up to, and including,

Choose the Best School 45

THE RIGHT SCHOOL (PERRY PRESCHOOL PROJECT)	THE WRONG SCHOOL (WEAK OR NO PRESCHOOL)
MORE INCOME **LESS CRIME**	MORE crime LESS INCOME
MORE HOME OWNERSHIP **LESS RELIANCE ON PUBLIC ASSISTANCE**	MORE reliance on public assistance Less home ownership
MORE EDUCATION **LESS UNMARRIED MOMS GIVING BIRTH**	MORE unmarried moms giving birth LESS EDUCATION

Figure 10.1 Results of the Wrong School and the Right School at Age Three to Four on Participants' Later Lives (in Their Late Twenties, Data from the Perry Preschool Project).

the senior year of high school.[11] When children attending classes taught by ineffective teachers in disorganized schools are reassigned to masterful teachers in well-run schools, the benefits are immediate, regardless of grade level, and the positive effects last for years.[12]

Fretting over the quality of schools is understandable, especially once the implications of making a bad decision are clear. The quality of a school is always important;[13] however, the influence of a school is most intense in the early years.[14] Parents today can homeschool or they can choose among three very different kinds of schools: public, private, and charter.

Strategy 10a = For Public Schools, Follow the Money
Strategy 10b = For Private Schools, Do Your Due Diligence
Strategy 10c = Avoid Charter Schools

STORY

The house sat across the street from an idyllic looking, immaculately maintained elementary school with a huge, bright blue "Welcome Students!" banner draped just above the front entrance. Rather than wait in long lines of cars to drop off her son before school and then pick him up after school, the mother considered how nice it would be to simply walk across the street. The school had a massive playground, with lots of open space.

Everything seemed to be perfect. In between unpacking boxes and setting up furniture, the mother and her son explored every inch of the playground. It was first grade and the boy did not know a single kid within 300 miles of his new home.

"School Preview Day," a time designated for parents to meet their child's teachers before the official opening of school, was only a few days away. Because friends and playmates constitute the quality of life for a child, mom and son were nervous about meeting the new teacher and getting a look at the inside of the school.

At first, the signs during School Preview Day seemed positive. The school's floors were sparklingly clean and the lockers were recently painted. However, when the mom and son went to pick up the schedule, the counselors did not seem organized and they continually shuffled through stacks of paper without saying much. The teachers they met in the hallway were more officious than friendly. The mother knew that in first grade, the single-most important factor in a child's development according to research is the child's relationship with his teacher.[15]

The mother managed to find her son's classroom and teacher—Mrs. Smith. Mrs. Smith was female, young, and had carefully coiffed hair. She stood outside the class entrance, greeting students and parents as they entered. As the mother and her son approached the door, Mrs. Smith started to smile and turn in their direction, but a cute, little girl in a bright red dress slipped in front of them.

"Hi Mrs. Smith. You are my new teacher!" said the little girl.

Mrs. Smith looked at the mom apologetically, then at the precious girl.

"Yes, I am," said Mrs. Smith. "Now go on in and sit down."

"And you know what?" continued the little girl.

"What?" said Mrs. Smith, with a hint of irritation in her voice.

"Today is my birthday!" said the little girl.

"Well, isn't that nice?" said Mrs. Smith, patting the little girl on the head and shaking her head from side to side. Then, she repeated, "Now go inside and sit down."

That was enough. Right there.

The mother had received ample information to determine that the school's climate was not child-friendly. Why weren't counselors ready for the first day of school? Why weren't teachers in the hall more friendly? What in the world was a woman who ignores a six-year-old's birthday doing teaching first grade?

The school's climate lacked the most important attribute—care.

The mom withdrew her son from the school and negotiated with the district to get him placed in a more welcoming place. She met with the principal at the second school who introduced her to several teachers. She selected a warm, delightful, whip-smart, veteran teacher and her son had a fantastic first-grade year.

STRATEGY 10A: FOR PUBLIC SCHOOLS, FOLLOW THE MONEY

The way that public schools are funded in the United States makes choosing a good one relatively straightforward. Here's the rule to follow if you want to enroll your child in a good public school: Move into the richest neighborhood that you can possibly afford. Well-run public schools in well-to-do neighborhoods in America may rival, or even surpass, the best private schools.[16]

If you are a parent who struggles to make ends meet, the rule is the same. Find the lowest-priced residence in the cheapest part of a wealthy neighborhood, and as long as the domicile is within the school's attendance boundary zone, the school must accept your child as a student.[17]

Once you identify the right school, an ideal situation would be finding a home within walking distance. Having the school nearby will save thousands of future trips in the car before your child learns to drive or is old enough to take the subway or bus by themselves. It also will save you from spending countless hours in long lines of cars, waiting to drop off or pick up your child.

Secondly, schools in rich neighborhoods tend to have fabulous playgrounds, so living near a school offers the advantage of having a handy, open play space available when your children are desperately energetic and want to "go play." An added advantage: The school maintains and updates playgrounds regularly at no additional cost to you. Finally, close proximity to school will make involvement in school-based activities, such as open houses, sports events, music and theater performances, meetings with teachers, booster clubs, and the Parent-Teacher Association, less cumbersome.

To reiterate, choose quality over convenience. Choose the best school over the most convenient school, even if the most convenient school happens to be next door and the best quality school is located across town.

The average breakdown for funding of public schools in the United States goes something like this (percentages vary depending on the state and locale in which you live):

- Federal contribution = 8%
- State contribution = 47%
- Local property taxes contribution = 45%[18]

Each state has its own formula for funding public schools. Because rich and poor public schools may receive comparable funding through federal and state allotments, often the differentiating factor is property taxes, which contribute, on average, 45 percent of the funds available for public schools. To put it succinctly: schools in rich areas have access to larger sums of money than those in poor areas.

Also, because children in wealthy schools tend to have influential, active, and wealthy parents, it is not unusual for booster groups in these neighborhoods to generate huge sums of money to support the arts, sports, field trips, or whatever is needed at school. The Center for American Progress estimates the contributions of parent-teacher organizations to be in the hundreds of millions of dollars nationwide, with most of it being generated by the wealthiest public schools.[19]

On average then, almost half of a school's funding is contingent upon the relative wealth of the people who live in the neighborhood in which the school is located.

Disparities in school funding can be readily apparent. A quick drive through neighborhoods and a glance at school buildings and adjacent grounds can say much about the wealth of a neighborhood, as well as serve as an indicator of a school's relative safety and academic reputation.

Figure 10.2 features photos of two high schools in the Dallas area—Thomas Jefferson High and Highland Park High. The Highland Park School District is actually adjacent to Dallas Independent School District, so that students living on one street might go to a Highland Park school, while students living on the next street would attend a school such as Thomas Jefferson.

Thomas Jefferson High has an illustrious heritage, though it was never an opulent school (top left). When the school was damaged by a tornado in 2019, it was moved into an abandoned, former junior high school (top right), Thomas Edison Junior High. As of this writing (three years later), the high school is still meeting in the old Thomas Edison Junior High Building and the tornado-damaged Thomas Jefferson has yet to reopen.[20]

Figure 10.2 Two High Schools in Dallas, Texas. *Source*: Photos by Jack Baines.

Highland Park High School (bottom left) is located in one of the most expensive neighborhoods in Texas. Highland Park has an impressive football stadium (bottom right), as well as multimillion-dollar indoor practice facilities for football and additional, separate facilities for other sports.[21] Indeed, the sports facilities at Highland Park are sufficiently posh that professional sports teams have asked to use the facilities on occasion when they are playing games in the area.[22]

Figure 10.3 compares Highland Park and Dallas in terms of property taxes, violent crime, median income, and average Scholastic Aptitude Test (SAT) scores.

Perhaps it might be surprising to learn that residents of the wealthy neighborhood of Highland Park pay a much lower property tax rate than households located outside of the school's attendance zone. This bears repeating: The property tax rate in one of the richest areas of Texas is significantly lower than the property tax rate in one of the poorest areas of Texas. The property tax rates in Highland Park are lower because the values of the houses are so

	Property taxes on a $600,000 home	Violent crime rate	Median household income	Average SAT score
Highland Park	✓ LOW $12,130[1]	✓ LOW Less than 1 (.44) violent crime for every 1000 people[2]	✓ HIGH $207,019[3]	✓ HIGH 1295[4]
Dallas	✗ HIGH $16,274[5]	✗ HIGH 8 violent crimes for every 1000 people (18 times higher than H.P.)[6]	✗ LOW $50,100[7]	✗ LOW 929[8]

[1] Dallas Central Appraisal District (2020). Property tax estimator for Highland Park. Dallas, Texas: DCAD. http://www.dallascad.org/TaxRateCalculator.aspx

[2] Texas Department of Public Safety (2020). Crime in Texas 2019. Austin, Texas: TDPS. https://www.dps.texas.gov/administration/crime_records/pages/crimestatistics.htm

[3] U.S. Census Bureau (2020). *Quick facts, Highland Park, Texas*. Washington, D.C.: U.S. Census Bureau. https://www.census.gov/quickfacts/highlandparktowntexas

[4] Texas Tribune (2020). *Public school explorer: Highland Park*. Austin, Texas: Texas Tribune. https://schools.texastribune.org/districts/highland-park-isd-dallas/highland-park-high-school/

[5] Dallas Central Appraisal District (2020). Property tax estimator for Dallas I.S.D. Dallas, Texas: DCAD. http://www.dallascad.org/TaxRateCalculator.aspx

[6] Goodman, M. (2020, August 11). As violent crime rises, Dallas Council conflicted on whom to blame. D Magazine. Dallas Texas: *D Magazine*. https://www.dmagazine.com/frontburner/2020/08/as-violent-crime-rises-dallas-council-conflicted-on-who-to-blame/

[7] U.S. Census Bureau (2020). *Quick facts, Dallas, Texas*. Washington, D.C.: U.S. Census Bureau. https://www.census.gov/quickfacts/fact/table/dallascitytexas/PST045219

[8] Texas Tribune (2020). *Public school explorer: Dallas ISD*. Austin, Texas: Texas Tribune. https://schools.texastribune.org/districts/dallas-isd/

Figure 10.3   Property Taxes, Crime, Income, and Average SAT in Two Cities in Texas.

much higher. A 2 percent rate on a $5,000,000 house in Highland Park would generate $100,000 in property taxes; a 2 percent rate on a $50,000 house in a poor, Dallas neighborhood would generate only $1000.

In addition to a lower property tax rate, residents of Highland Park also experience less violent crime and students in Highland Park schools enjoy stellar SAT scores, well above the national mean.

Meanwhile, households located in Dallas Independent School District, on average, earn about $157,000 less than households in Highland Park, and they live in one of the most violent areas of the country.[23] Students in Dallas post below-average SAT scores, but if their parents could somehow move across school boundary lines into Highland Park, the test scores of their children could possibly improve by hundreds of points, their property tax rates would fall, and they would be less troubled by crime.

Fifty years of data from the National Center for Education Statistics attest that schools in wealthy neighborhoods consistently have the following advantages:

1. Few disciplinary problems
2. High student achievement
3. Up-to-date technology
4. Better availability of counselors, librarians, nurses, support staff
5. Access to a more advanced and extensive curriculum
6. Safer, more modern buildings[24]

In contrast, schools located in areas of high poverty may have to confront myriad challenges, beginning with the physical condition of the school, itself. Recent reports of urban schools located in poor neighborhoods have reported buildings with no heat during winter, unsafe water, rampant mold, poor ventilation, and animal and insect infestations.[25]

Schools in high-poverty neighborhoods tend to have older, less well-maintained buildings, fewer experienced teachers, more disciplinary problems, limited access to services, less up-to-date technology, and reduced access to an advanced curriculum, such as Advanced Placement (AP) courses in high school.[26]

Because schools in wealthy neighborhoods have larger budgets, they can afford to pay slightly higher salaries.[27] Thus, teachers and administrators who have been proven effective tend to migrate to safer, higher-achieving schools where they encounter fewer bureaucratic and community hassles and might enjoy higher pay or better benefits.[28]

Nationally, the top, high-achieving public schools are disproportionately suburban and affluent. Between 2000 and 2015, funding for most public schools remained static while funding for the top-performing public schools increased by more than 30 percent.[29]

Of course, funding for public schools is highly idiosyncratic; no two states or localities are alike. In terms of federal/state/local funding, consider differences in these four states:

California 9% federal/ *58% state*/ 33% local
Michigan 9% federal/ 31% state/ *61% local*
New York 5% federal/ 41% state/ 54% local
Texas *11% federal*/39% state /50% local

One might think that disparities between rich and poor schools might be less obvious in states, such as California and Michigan, where the federal and state government combine to fund up to 70 percent of basic costs. Yet, even in these states, the local supplement plays a critical role in determining funding.

As in Texas, the lowest local property tax rates in California can be found in the state's wealthiest neighborhoods. For example, the effective property tax rate of Palo Alto, the neighborhood surrounding Stanford University, is the lowest in the entire state,[30] despite the fact that the median price of a home in Palo Alto is over three million dollars.[31]

The pattern becomes problematic in the poorest areas of California. For example, the property tax rate of Arvin, California, a humble, small city southeast of Bakersfield, where the average price of a house is only $185,250,[32] is more than triple the property tax rate of wealthy Palo Alto.[33]

As wealthy neighborhoods have gotten more expensive in California, poor areas have become even more impoverished. The phenomenon of taxing the poor at higher rates than the rich has become standard operating procedure throughout many parts of the United States. As property values decline in poor neighborhoods, taxes have to be raised just to keep school doors open. When property values soar in wealthy neighborhoods, taxes can be cut without reducing the money that goes to schools.

Figure 10.4 describes the neo-feudal, property tax phenomenon as it manifests in two cities in Michigan. Residents of the poorest city in the state, Detroit, actually pay more than double the property tax rate of residents of Rochester Hills, one of the wealthiest areas in the country.[34] Not only is the tax rate higher in Detroit, but the violent crime rate is more than twenty times the violent crime rate of Rochester Hills. Yet, median income in Detroit is $60,000 less and SAT scores are hundreds of points lower. Rochester Hills wins in all categories; Detroit loses in all categories, including the property tax rate.

The vast differences in school quality found between schools located in rich and poor neighborhoods in Michigan, California, and Texas are not unusual but are the norm nationwide.[35]

Choose the Best School

CITY	PROPERTY TAX ON A $200,000 HOME	VIOLENT CRIME RATE	MEDIAN HOUSEHOLD INCOME	AVERAGE SAT SCORE
DETROIT	✗ HIGH $14,000[i]	✗ HIGH 21 violent crimes for every 1000 people[ii]	✗ LOW $29,481[iii]	✗ LOW 822[iv] (King High)
ROCHESTER HILLS	✓ LOW $6422[v]	✓ LOW Less than 1 (.7) violent crime for every 1000 people[vi]	✓ HIGH $90,961[vii]	✓ HIGH 1128[viii] (Stoney Creek High)

[i] Michigan Department of Treasury (2020). Michigan taxes: Property Tax Estimator for Wayne County/Detroit City Schools. Lansing, MI: Michigan Department of Treasury. https://treas-secure.state.mi.us/ptestimator/PTEstimator.asp

[ii] Davis Law Group (2020). Violent crime statistics in Detroit. Detroit, MI: Davis Law Group. https://www.michigancriminallawyer.com/violent-crime-statistics-detroit/

[iii] U.S. Census Bureau (2020). Quick facts, Detroit city. Washington, D.C.: U.S. Census Bureau. https://www.census.gov/quickfacts/detroitcitymichigan

[iv] Mack, J. (2019, May 20). 52 Michigan high schools where less than 5% test as college-ready. Detroit, MI: MLIVE. https://www.mlive.com/news/2017/06/52_michigan_high_schools_were.html

[v] Michigan Department of Treasury (2020). Michigan taxes: Property Tax Estimator for Oakland County/Rochester Community Schools. Lansing, MI: Michigan Department of Treasury. https://treas-secure.state.mi.us/ptestimator/PTEstimator.asp

[vi] Mack, J. (2019, October 3). Which Michigan communities had the highest violent-crime rate in 2018? Detroit, MI: MLIVE. https://www.mlive.com/news/g66l-2019/10/2c291700cd8326/which-michigan-communities-had-the-highest-violentcrime-rate-in-2018.html

[vii] U.S. Census Bureau (2020). Quick facts, Rochester Hills. Washington, D.C.: U.S. Census Bureau. https://www.census.gov/quickfacts/fact/table/rochesterhillscitymichigan,rochestercityindiana,detroitcitymichigan/PST045219

[viii] Stoney Creek High School (2020, January 30). *Annual education report letter*. Rochester Hills, MI: Rochester Community Schools. https://www.rochester.k12.mi.us/pages/335/stoneycreek

Figure 10.4 Property Taxes, Crime, Income, and SAT Scores in Two Cities in Michigan.

Public schools in New York follow similar patterns, with richer schools benefiting from an array of factors—more money, higher achievement, better school infrastructure, less crime, fewer problems, and lower property tax

	POUGHKEEPSIE HIGH SCHOOL (POUGHKEEPSIE, NEW YORK) HIGH POVERTY	JERICHO HIGH SCHOOL (JERICHO, NEW YORK) MIDDLE CLASS
ECONOMICALLY DISADVANTAGED	75% ☹	13% ☺
STUDENTS SCORING THE HIGHEST SCORE (5) ON REGENT'S LANGUAGE ARTS	12% ☹	85% ☺
STUDENTS SCORING THE HIGHEST SCORE (5) ON REGENT'S EXAM ALGEBRA II	4% ☹	73% ☺
GRADUATION RATE	57% ☹	99% ☺
STUDENTS WITH DISABILITIES	17% ☹	12% ☺
CHRONIC ABSENTEEISM	42% ☹	12% ☺
PERCENT INEXPERIENCED TEACHERS (DISTRICT)	33% ☹	12% ☺
OUT-OF-FIELD TEACHERS (STATE AVERAGE)	23% ☹	2% ☺
DISTRICT EXPENDITURES PER STUDENT	$21,235 ☹	$33,445 ☺

Figure 10.5 Student and Teacher Characteristics in Two High Schools in New York.

rates. However, the focus of figure 10.5 is on characteristics of students and teachers in two schools—one poor and one middle class.

In schools that educate large numbers of students living in poverty, such as Poughkeepsie High, student absenteeism and the number of students with disabilities tend to be higher than in wealthy or middle-class schools, like Jericho. States allocate money to schools based upon attendance rates, so high absenteeism inevitably leads to lower funding.

Because children with special needs can cost three times as much to educate as non-special-needs children, a higher incidence of special-needs children translates into fewer instructional dollars spent on students who are not in special education.[36] Special education, by law, must secure the "least restrictive environment" for each child and providing the least restricted environment can be quite expensive.[37]

In addition, poor schools are three times more likely to employ new and out-of-field or uncertified teachers, while middle-class schools, like Jericho High School, tend to retain experienced teachers, who are more likely to be certified in the subject areas they are assigned to teach.[38] Inexperienced teachers are "often assigned to schools that teachers with more seniority avoid."[39]

Undoubtedly, superb schools exist in poor neighborhoods, but with the current system of funding, the probability of finding a great school decreases as the wealth of a neighborhood declines. Ohio rates every school in the state using a ranking system of A to F, with A being the highest possible score and F the lowest. In a recent year, the state rated all of their wealthiest schools as deserving an A or B and rated most of their poorest schools as F. None of the poorest schools received an A; only 4 percent of the poorest schools received a B.[40]

Again, the best advice for selecting a great public school in the United States is to "follow the money."

STORY

Parents who understand the value of a good education can go to great lengths to get their children enrolled in the right public school. Kelly Williams Bolar was a parent with two daughters who lived in central Akron, one of the poorest areas of Ohio.[41] The neighborhood near her children's public school was not only low-performing but located in an area of high crime and violence. Kelly's father lived in Copley, Ohio, in a lovely, safe neighborhood near an affluent public school named Copley-Fairlawn Middle School.

Using her father's address, Kelly enrolled her two daughters in Copley-Fairlawn and they performed quite well.[42] However, the school discovered the ruse and asked the police to arrest Kelly for "grand theft" for trying to "steal" an education for her children.[43] The judge in the case found Kelly guilty and sentenced her to two concurrent five-year terms in prison. After Kelly spent nine days in jail and after a flood of negative national media attention, then-governor John Kasich reduced the felony convictions to misdemeanors.[44]

Kelly Williams-Bolar understood the value of a good education, so deserves kudos for trying to place her children in a high-quality school.

However, because most public schools are reliant upon property taxes for their funding, they tend to be vigilant about restricting enrollment to individuals who actually live within school boundary lines. Certainly, the system as it currently exists is stacked against poor families who lack mobility.

If Kelly could have found a modest place to live within the Copley school district, there would have been no case and no trial. With the way the current system works in most states, for parents who want their child to attend a great public school, sometimes moving is the only option.

STRATEGY 10B: FOR PRIVATE SCHOOLS, DO YOUR DUE DILIGENCE

Private schools in the United States have a long and illustrious history. The Boston Latin School was established in 1635, 141 years before the signing of the Declaration of Independence.[45] Collegiate School, in New York City, was chartered three years later, in 1638, and like The Boston Latin School, still enrolls students today—mostly from well-heeled, well-connected families. Gaining admission to such private schools can be challenging.

The education at the best private schools tends to be unapologetically rigorous and quite expensive, but one reason admissions are so selective is because results are impressive. Students from private schools such as Boston Latin School and Collegiate School tend to have significantly higher rates of acceptance into the most prestigious colleges and universities in the United States.[46]

Today, about 10 percent of children in the United States attend a private school.[47] For families who can afford the tuition, private schools can provide exemplary experiences, but due diligence in the form of a thorough fact-finding investigation is required. Because the gap between the best and worst private schools is enormous, extreme caution must be used, particularly when considering new and unproven private schools.

Typically, salaries for teachers at private schools are up to a third lower than salaries for public school teachers. In 2020, teachers at public schools earned an average salary of $57,900 while teachers in private school earned an average salary of $45,300.[48] Teacher churn (teachers quitting or taking jobs elsewhere) at private schools is higher than public schools but lower than charter schools.[49]

Perhaps the best way to get a sense of the private school universe is to examine a few, well-established private schools in specific areas of the country. For private schools, being well-established is important, as closures and bankruptcies have soared in recent years. Since the 1960s, enrollment in Catholic schools has declined by 65 percent.[50] A flurry of recent reports confirm that many private schools, religious or nonreligious, remain on "precarious financial footing."[51]

So, before signing a contract with a private school, make sure that the school's infrastructure, meaning their classrooms, administrative offices, library, gym, labs, furniture, and financial status, are solid. An established private school should be preferred over a new school, simply because new schools have higher probabilities of closure and, when they close, they take your tuition money with them.[52]

Table 10.1 offers a glimpse of tuition and mission statements for pairs of private schools in four different states as of 2022. As shown in the table, tuition costs at nonreligious and nondenominational, "Christian values" private schools tend to be more expensive than private schools affiliated with a specific religion, such as Catholic, Episcopal, or Jewish. That is because religious schools typically receive financial support from their affiliated religious organizations.

Schools that advocate "Christian values" usually welcome any faiths, including nonbelievers and those who profess belief in other faiths. As a result, most nondenominational private schools receive no additional funding from churches or other organizations.

As can be seen from figure 10.6, the most prestigious, well-regarded private schools are pricey, indeed. At the high end, the cost to a family with only two children at Trinity School in New York City is almost $120,000, and Trinity is nowhere near the most expensive private school in New York City. At the low end, costs for a family with two children at Bishop Lynch High School in Dallas is about $40,000.

At private schools one should always expect "additional fees" over the course of a year—for sports, books, club participation, field trips, award ceremonies, and any number of events, so actual costs will be greater than the tuition costs noted in the initial paperwork. While additional expenses also occur in public schools (a few public schools on the West Coast have started requiring parents to pay for their children's participation in sports), the pain seems more severe at schools that already charge high tuition.

The mission statements of private schools are useful in considering whether or not your child would fit with the student body. The mention of *global travel* in its mission statement means that students at Trinity School in New York City likely go abroad for part of the school year; Cranbrook Schools in Detroit mentions *residential* in their mission statement, which means that a certain percentage of their students live on campus 24/7 and that their parents likely live out of state or out of the country.

While Frankel Jewish Academy asks that students dedicate themselves to "Jewish . . . peoplehood, and the State of Israel," Greenhill Academy in

Table 10.1 Private School Comparisons in New York, California, Texas, and Michigan

Location	Annual Tuition	Mission Statement Excerpts
New York City: Trinity School (Nondenominational Christian)	$56,770, but "additional expenses for textbooks, field trips, etc."[i]	"Since 1709, Trinity has provided a world-class education to its students with rigorous academics and outstanding programs in athletics, the arts, peer leadership, and global travel."[ii]
New York City: Loyola School (Catholic)	$42,600 plus about $2,000 in additional fees[iii]	"As a Catholic, independent, coeducational, college Loyola School challenges its young men and women to become intellectually fulfilled, open to growth, religious, loving, and committed to doing justice."[iv]
Dallas: Greenhill School (No Religious Affiliation)	$33,230[v] (includes lunch, but not additional fees)	"Greenhill School . . . strives for excellence; values individuality; fosters a passion for learning; promotes the balanced development of mind, body, and character; encourages service; and instills a respect for others."[vi]
Dallas: Bishop Lynch High School (Catholic)	$18,800[vii] (includes breakfast and lunch, but not additional fees)	"Bishop Lynch promotes the development of the total person by bringing together a diverse community in a rigorous, college preparatory environment where students are taught to strive for excellence, seek truth, and work for justice in the world."[viii]
Oakland, CA: College Prep High School (No Religious Affiliation)	$48,300 plus $1500 additional fees[ix]	"We challenge our students to engage deeply in learning, appreciate one another, and grow into adults who are intellectually adventurous, ethically sure-footed, and generous of heart and spirit."[x]
Oakland, CA: St. Paul's Episcopal School (K–8)	$34,230, but "facilities and after school program costs are additional"[xi]	"As part of our Episcopal tradition, we develop independence, respect, empathy, fairness, and the moral imperative to serve others and care for our planet."[xii]
Detroit, MI: Cranbrook Schools (No Religious Affiliation)	$36,200 plus additional fees[xiii]	"Cranbrook Schools . . . motivate students from diverse backgrounds to strive for intellectual, creative, and physical excellence, to develop a deep appreciation for the arts and different cultures, and to employ the technological tools of our modern age."[xiv]

(Continued)

Table 10.1 Private School Comparisons in New York, California, Texas, and Michigan (Continued)

Location	Annual Tuition	Mission Statement Excerpts
Detroit, MI: Frankel Jewish Academy	$28,000[xv]	"Frankel Jewish Academy is . . . pursuing academic excellence and Jewish literacy. We inspire students to think critically, creatively, and compassionately; to dedicate themselves to Jewish tradition, peoplehood, and the State of Israel."[xvi]

[i]Trinity School (2021). *Admissions, 2020-21 Academic year.* www.trinityschoolnyc.org
[ii]Trinity School (2021). *History of Trinity School.* www.trinityschoolnyc.org
[iii]Loyola School (2021). *Tuition and financial aid resources.* www.loyolanyc.org
[iv]Loyola School (2021). *Discover Loyola.* www.loyolanyc.org.
[v]Greenhill School (2021). *Tuition schedule.* www.greenhill.org
[vi]Greenhill School (2021). *Mission statement.* www.greenhill.org
[vii]Bishop Lynch High School (2021). *Tuition and fees.* www.bishoplynch.org
[viii]Bishop Lynch High School (2021). *Our heritage and mission.* www.bishoplynch.org
[ix]College Prep Academy (2021). *Tuition and fees.* www.college-prep.org
[x]College Prep Academy (2021). *Our mission.* www.college-prep.org
[xi]St. Paul's Episcopal School (2021). *Tuition for the school year.* www.spes.org
[xii]St. Paul's Episcopal School (2021). *Mission & values.* www.spes.org
[xiii]Cranbrook Schools (2021). *Affording Cranbrook.* www.schools.cranbrook.edu
[xiv]Cranbrook Schools (2021). *Mission statement.* www.schools.cranbrook.edu
[xv]Frankel Jewish Academy (2021). *Paying for FJA.* www.frankelja.org
[xvi]Frankel Jewish Academy (2021). *Mission & core values.* www.frankelja.org

Dallas uses terms, such as *diverse* and *individuality* in its mission statement, indicating a nonreligious and "looser" curricular approach.

Research[53] has found that private schools differ from public schools in terms of diversity and size; however, there may be surprisingly little difference in terms of student achievement, especially when the parental income of students attending the schools are comparable.[54]

Perhaps the biggest challenge with private schools is that admission is not guaranteed. Just because you want your child to go to a high-prestige private school does not mean that he/she will gain entrance, as the best schools are highly competitive. For example, Trinity School in New York City has an acceptance rate of under 10 percent and almost all of the parents are wealthy and their children very smart.

The acceptance rate is 25 percent at Greenhill in Dallas; 36 percent at Cranbrook in Detroit.[55] So, if your child can get into one of the best private schools—congratulations for having both deep financial assets and brilliant children. If your child cannot get into one of the best private schools and you want your child to attend a private school, you will need to do some homework.

Go on a tour, speak with the headmaster and counselor, find out the exact costs, chat with teachers and coaches, visit the library, confer with current students and parents, then decide.

Strategy 10

DIFFERENCES	RESEARCH FINDINGS[i]
DIVERSITY IS LOWER 	70% of students in private schools are white; 50% of students in public schools are white. Private schools employ far fewer nonwhite teachers than public schools[ii] 2% of students in private schools are special needs children; 14% of students in public schools are special needs children[iii]
SIZE IS  **SMALLER**	Most (83%) private schools are located in cities or suburbs; public schools are located in all areas Private schools tend to be smaller at every grade level with an average student body of 166 students; the average student body of a public school is 526 students.
FAMILY ATTRIBUTES ARE STRONGER 	Students in private schools come from wealthier backgrounds Students in private schools tend to have higher achievement scores. However, in studies that have controlled for demographic differences, such as wealth, the "presumably advantageous 'private school effect' disappears."[iv] More students in private schools come from two-parent households Parents of students in private schools tend to be better educated

---

[i] National Center for Education Statistics (2020). *Public and private school comparison.* Washington, D.C.: NCES. https://nces.ed.gov/fastfacts/display.asp?id=55. Much of the data on the list below derives from this document.

[ii] National Center for Education Statistics (2019). Teacher characteristics and trends. Washington, D.C.: NCES. https://nces.ed.gov/fastfacts/display.asp?id=28

[iii] Samuels, C. (2018, August 2). How private schools and districts partner up on special education. *Education Week.* https://www.edweek.org/ew/articles/2018/08/02/how-private-schools-and-districts-partner-up.html

[iv] Lubienski, S. T., & Lubienski, C. (2006). School Sector and Academic Achievement: A Multilevel Analysis of NAEP Mathematics Data. *American Educational Research Journal,* 43(4), 651–698.

Figure 10.6   How Private Schools Differ from Public Schools in Terms of Diversity, Size, and Family Attributes.

STORY

In general, state laws do not require private schools to hire certified, subject-area experts as teachers.[56] A few years ago, a father who taught at a private school, started having trouble with his son's eighth-grade math teacher. Since the father actually taught at the same private school, he investigated the math teacher's background and discovered that not only did she not have a degree in mathematics, but she never even graduated from college.[57] The inept teacher, who was the school's only math teacher for eighth grade, significantly set back the son's education in math, a deficit from which it took years to recover.

On the other hand, the father who taught at the school was a brilliant writer and an inspiring teacher who held two advanced degrees from highly regarded universities. Both the father and the incompetent math teacher worked at the same school. That is why, with private schools, parents must perform their due diligence.

STRATEGY 10C: AVOID CHARTER SCHOOLS

There is little difference between nonprofit and profit-centered charter schools.[58] Both tend to be designed from the inception to generate maximum revenue so that their owner-operators can pay themselves well.[59] Most money that goes to owner-operators is money taken away from potential expenditures that would benefit students, such as instruction or facilities.

Even administrators at KIPP, one of the most celebrated charter school franchises, pay themselves hundreds of thousands of dollars in annual salary more than their public school counterparts, and they give themselves numerous additional perks, such as extended vacations to Disney World and other resorts.[60]

The two owners of the EPIC charter school chain in Oklahoma, a "nonprofit" organization, paid themselves $10 million of public money, though neither served as a teacher or administrator in any of their schools.[61] At the same time the owner/operators of EPIC were paying themselves millions of dollars, the salaries of public school teachers in Oklahoma were the lowest in the nation.[62]

Most charter schools provide absolutely no benefits to employees and are lightly regulated, so perhaps it is no surprise that many charter school owner-operators have become millionaires.[63] Also, as a recent investigative report found, charter schools tend to be located in substandard buildings, feature few (if any) services, and are not required to provide the "basics," including special education services, counseling, college/career advisement, libraries, nurses, clubs, science labs, and sports.[64]

One of the problems with charter schools is that many do not stick around. To date, more than a million children have been displaced by charter schools that have gone under.[65] Indeed, many charter schools do not last a year; one in five closes within three years.[66]

Charters also can be selective in admissions. So, if a child is not of the right religion, ethnicity, or gender or if they lack a specific ability or disposition, they may have zero chance of being admitted.[67] Indeed, the highest achieving charter schools also tend to impose the most selective admissions.[68] The following are six reasons to avoid charter schools.

1. About half of charter schools close within a decade[69]
2. Many charter schools are discriminatory in admissions[70]
3. Teachers at charter schools are not required to be certified or to hold degrees in their teaching fields.[71] Also, charter schools pay lower salaries and are likely to pay no benefits, so they tend to attract less qualified teachers[72]
4. Charter schools are largely unregulated[73]
5. Charter schools may not serve students with disabilities[74]
6. Charter schools may not provide student services, such as counseling, sports, clubs, tutors, nurses, or libraries[75]

In terms of achievement, some students enrolled in charter schools perform better than students in traditional public schools, but most perform worse.[76] A recent study concisely sums the current state of charter schools:

> The charter movement has come to reflect the business values of its philanthropic backers: many charter schools in New Orleans and elsewhere are more McDonald's than artisanal eatery. Like fast-food chains, KIPP and other charter-management organizations often rely on cheap, transient labor, much of it supplied by Teach for America, which gives recent college graduates only five weeks of training before placing them in schools.[77]

The vast majority of Teach for America (TFA) students, for example, readily admit that they want to leave the classroom as soon as they possibly can after their teaching obligations are finished in two years.[78] While many TFA teachers are smart and well-meaning, most have had little to no preparation in classroom management, child development, or effective instruction.[79]

If your child's teacher is TFA, know that they are probably smart, but untrained and inexperienced.[80] Because of low pay and substandard school infrastructure, charter schools have the highest rates of teacher and administrative turnover of any school and offer few, if any, student services.[81] If possible, avoid charter schools.

STORY

A student named Dorothy asked to be added to an English Methods class at a university in early September after the semester had already begun. The class was focused on instructional strategies for teaching English to high school students. The professor always asked students to introduce themselves and to say something about their background and why they wanted to become teachers of English.

During her self-introduction, Dorothy revealed that she had a bachelor's degree in business from a local college, had worked for twenty years as a legal secretary, and had just taken a job as a teacher of high school English at a newly opened charter school near downtown.

She did not really want to teach, she said, but the salary was better than what she was making as a legal secretary. Dorothy also revealed that my course was the first course in education she had ever taken.

Dorothy was smart and ambitious, but she knew precious little about literature, writing, language, instructional strategies, curriculum—or even, how to interact with students. She had absolutely no previous experience working with children.

A few days after her first class as a teacher, Dorothy confided in the professor that, in recent days, she had physically restrained a few students by pushing them back into their seats and forcing them to sit down. Also, she had gotten into a "shoving match" with an administrator in the lunchroom, and gotten into a fistfight with a parent during a conference after school.

The professor offered advice ("do not attempt to physically overpower students, administrators, or parents—just talk with them"), encouraged her to return to the university class, and promised to work with her to help her get a handle on the situation.

However, Dorothy never returned to class, though she called often, looking for help. In the professor's last conversation with her, Dorothy said that her charter school had lost more than half of its students and that most of the teachers had quit because the school was "a madhouse, in a continual state of chaos." In addition, the security officer at the school had been charged with sexually assaulting a student and the delivery of Dorothy's most recent paycheck had been indefinitely delayed.

Strategy 11

Select the Right Teacher

A group of Harvard economists has estimated a good teacher's value to students in a single year to be worth a million dollars.[1] The Stanford economist Eric Hanushek agrees that an effective teacher has significant economic value, but places the annual effect at closer to two million dollars (the incompetent teacher decreases collective future earnings of students by a million dollars while the accomplished teacher increases collective future earnings by a million).[2]

Hanushek formulated his hypothesis using one teacher and a single class of twenty students.[3] However, because elementary teachers often have classes of thirty or more and because secondary teachers may instruct more than 200 students every day,[4] the financial benefits of being taught by an accomplished teacher may be even greater than what either Hanushek or Chetty have initially calculated.

Teaching effectively is both an art and science.[5] A teacher must teach a lesson so that the disequilibrium that accompanies learning is mitigated by excitement or keen interest.[6] If the lesson is too easy, a student becomes bored and learns nothing; if the lesson is too hard, the student may become frustrated or shut down.[7]

The teacher must know the level of the student so she/he can create lessons that are sufficiently engaging and worthwhile, not too difficult and not too easy. Flow is the optimal state for learning, where the student's abilities are a perfect match for the difficulty of the task at hand.[8]

The Russian psychologist Lev Vygotsky called the optimal space for learning the "zone of proximal development."[9] "The zone" involves tasks that a child can achieve at the limits of his/her ability, but only with the help of an expert, usually a teacher or parent.

In many schools, particularly struggling public schools, there may be a rage for uniformity and consistency for delivery of the curriculum. Administrators at such schools often demand that every student receive the same education, meaning the same curriculum delivered in the same way, irrespective of aptitude.

Certainly, a lockstep approach makes bookkeeping easier, but the downside is that such an approach is antithetical to learning. Consider being a teacher of music and that you have a range of talents among your students in class. One student may be a veritable Mozart while another may be a tone-deaf child who has never listened to a single piece of music.

Obviously, the curriculum that would help the budding Mozart would be radically different from the one that might help the music-less, tone-deaf child. The job of a teacher is to *challenge students where they are* and help lead them to *where they could be*.

Because each student has such different talents and dispositions, teaching effectively is always complex and demanding. Teachers must negotiate challenges and obstructions moment-by-moment. They must recall student characteristics on-the-spot, deliver instruction, monitor student understanding, answer questions, think up examples, evaluate instructional effectiveness, anticipate and correct student misbehavior, interact with technology, ad infinitum.

While it is widely accepted that doctors and nurses experience extreme levels of stress, recently psychologists have found that the stress levels of teachers are comparable.[10] More than half of teachers report high stress daily, which compromises "health, sleep, quality of life, and teaching performance."[11]

Trying to determine the exact number of decisions that an "average teacher" makes is difficult, but researchers have hypothesized that it is somewhere between one and four every minute, perhaps several thousand decisions a day.[12]

In addition to making decisions regarding planning and assignments, teachers communicate with parents and administrators, continually assess student work, perform bookkeeping tasks (tardies, absences, lunch money, permissions, Individualized Educational Plans, Code 504 modifications), enforce administrative policies (dress code, academic policies, school-wide directives), and regularly meet with special educators, counselors, and fellow teachers.

In describing the challenges of being a teacher, the U.S. government's publication, *Occupational Handbook*, states:

> Some schools have large classes and lack important teaching tools, such as current technology and up-to-date textbooks. Occasionally, teachers must cope with unmotivated or disrespectful students.[13]

Any former teacher could personally attest to a lack of current technology and up-to-date books in schools. Also, any teacher knows that they must cope with unmotivated or disrespectful students as a matter of course, every minute of every day.

It is the rare child who would place doing problems in mathematics in their top ten of "favorite activities." Perhaps the two most essential aspects of a teacher's job are motivating students to learn and making learning as enjoyable as possible.[14] With the intellectual, social, and moral development of children riding on their spontaneous responses, teachers must remain constantly aware and engaged.[15]

The next three subchapters make the case that you do not have to passively accept the teacher to whom your child has been assigned. Taking an active role in finding the best teacher, tutor, or coach for your child is well worth the effort.

Strategy 11a = Actively Seek Out the Best
Strategy 11b = Insist on Honesty and Enthusiasm
Strategy 11c = Consider the Teacher's Education and Experience

STORY

There was an emergency-certified teacher who was having an ongoing battle with a ninth-grade student named Rita.[16] Instead of doing worksheets as the teacher demanded, Rita would type on her laptop.

When Rita would not give up her laptop, the teacher sent her to the assistant principal who sentenced Rita to in-house suspension. When the in-house suspension officer tried to wrestle Rita's laptop from her grasp on the first day, she resisted and pushed him away. The in-house suspension officer claimed that Rita's push constituted assault and called the police.

The police came to the school, placed Rita in handcuffs at the school, and drove her to the police station. The school eventually dropped the assault charge, and Rita's mother wisely moved her to a different school.

At the new school, Rita's mother actively sought out the best possible teachers. Rita's new teacher had a master's degree from a state university and twenty years' experience. Right away, the teacher suggested Rita be tested for special education. A psychologist found that Rita had Asperger's syndrome, which typically involves hypersensitivity, difficulty with social interactions, and the ability to focus with great intensity.[17]

Subsequent testing revealed that Rita had an IQ of 140, which allowed her to enroll in gifted courses. Rita still had challenges at school, but with the help of her new teacher, she earned all A's and eventually made some friends. During her junior year at the new school, Rita took the PSAT and made a perfect score, resulting in scholarship offers from several prestigious institutions.

With the teacher at her previous school, Rita could have gone to jail, would have probably flunked out of high school, and likely faced a bleak future. In a different school with a different teacher, Rita not only stayed out of jail, but she also graduated from high school, went to college on a "full ride," and started a happy, successful life after college. The difference between the two scenarios? One teacher.

STRATEGY 11A: ACTIVELY SEEK OUT THE BEST

Most people associate the name Benjamin Bloom with "Bloom's taxonomy," the big theory that cognition has six levels—knowledge, comprehension, application, analysis, synthesis, and evaluation.[18] Bloom also studied the potential effects of various instructional strategies on student learning. In his famous article, "The two-sigma problem," Bloom presents an incredible finding: Placing a child with an effective tutor in a one-on-one situation is, by far, the most effective instructional strategy of all.[19]

While an average student with no tutor might progress very little, Bloom found that an average student with an effective tutor could soar into the top 2 percent of class.[20] I want to emphasize that finding. With the help of a good tutor, an average student can become a high achiever, in the top 2 percent of all students.

The potential role of a tutor is especially pertinent if you find that your child is having difficulty in a particular subject, such as foreign language or science, or wants to excel in a certain activity, such as tennis or the trumpet.

Generally, in statistics, the larger the effect size, the larger the positive impact on learning. Bloom found that nine of the top ten most powerful influences on achievement, the variables with the greatest effect size, related to the quality of the teacher.[21] The top ten instructional techniques and their effect sizes are as follows:

1. One-on-one instruction, 2.0
2. Reinforcement from the teacher, 1.2
3. Responding to feedback from the teacher. 1.0
4. Teacher explanations, 1.0
5. Participation in class, 1.0
6. Time on task, 1.0
7. Improved reading skills, 1.0
8. Cooperative learning, .8

9. Graded homework, .8
10. Classroom environment/ morale, .6

One hundred years of research confirm that a single teacher can influence not only achievement and grades but also a child's confidence, motivation, character, self-regulation, persistence, college enrollment, empathy, adaptability, and future dispositions toward learning.[22] Quite a list.

The ideal teacher is one who has genuine affection for your child, someone who takes an active interest, an individual who is tenderhearted, kind, and patient. The essential role of care is well established not only in clinical studies but through the evidence of the real lives of loved and unloved children.[23] Care isn't a fluffy add-on; it is essential.

As mentioned in discussions of previous strategies in this book, unloved or socially isolated children have much higher rates of illness and premature death than children who have been cared for.[24] According to medical professionals, "loneliness and social isolation are twice as harmful to physical and mental health as obesity."[25]

Research confirms that caring teachers also tend to be the most effective teachers.[26]

STORY

The saddest studies in education have to do with what happens when affection is withheld. (See the Skeels studies discussed with Strategy 1.) In studies of orphanages where care is minimal or nonexistent, results inevitably find lower achievement, depression, belligerence, and "outright violent interpersonal behavior."[27] Neglect in childhood is associated with permanent damage to the brain, while a loving environment builds healthy brains with strong, highly connective neural pathways.[28]

Abused children typically struggle to develop empathy and altruism as adults.[29] Developing a sense of morality and learning how to be happy also seem to be contingent on the presence or absence of early care.[30]

However, it would be wrong to suggest that neglected and abused children are predestined for a life of misery. Indeed, any caring adult—an aunt, friend, or teacher—can help a troubled child develop resilience and increase the probability of living a happy and meaningful life.

Quinn was a friend and a teacher in one of the poorest school districts in Florida. A few years ago, he spoke to me about a student, named Arthur, in one of his classes. He thought Arthur was brilliant, but he was also rebellious, angry, and fiercely independent. Arthur showed up to eat the school lunch, but usually skipped classes and often did nothing when he attended.

One day, Quinn had a chat with Arthur after school and discovered that he was homeless. Arthur's mom had a new boyfriend and the new boyfriend had kicked Arthur out of the trailer, so he had been sleeping at his friend's houses or in the local park. Quinn invited Arthur to stay with him and his family (he was married and he and his wife had two children) whenever he needed to.

Arthur spent a lot of time with Quinn's family, and when Quinn took a new job in Texas, he invited Arthur to come live with them. Arthur agreed and posted high-enough grades as a senior at his new Texas high school to receive a few full scholarships for college. Eventually, Arthur got his bachelor's degree, then a master's, and finally a doctorate. Arthur had a tough upbringing, but with Quinn and his family's support, he had a home and a reason to wake up in the morning.

STRATEGY 11B: INSIST ON HONESTY AND ENTHUSIASM

The definition of apathy is "lack of feeling or emotion."[31] When you ponder the times you have been most bored in your life, perhaps your mind returns to middle school, high school, or college when you had the misfortune of enduring a class taught by a dull, passionless teacher, someone who was "just going through the motions."

Over the years, Gallup has conducted more than five million surveys concerning what students think about school. The results reveal that about half of the students in grades five to twelve find school boring most of the time.[32] Some critics rightly blame the vapid school culture that has been built around standardized testing for the decline in student engagement.[33] Whatever its source, there is no denying that boredom is rampant, particularly in secondary schools.

To fend off boredom, no cure is known to work better than enthusiasm.[34] About enthusiasm J.M. Parry writes:

> We talk and act as though comfort and luxury were the prime necessities of our existence, but for fulfillment what we really need is something to be enthusiastic about.[35]

Some parents may view the idea that enthusiasm can influence achievement skeptically, but real enthusiasm is a potent and precious commodity.[36] A teacher's enthusiasm is one of the few phenomena in the world that can help move a child's level of excitement from zilch to "maybe I'm interested."[37] Many studies have found enthusiasm to be "the most powerful unique predictor of students' intrinsic motivation and vitality."[38]

A vital, motivated child is preferable to a listless, unresponsive child in countless ways. A child's enthusiasm improves behavior, assures emotional engagement, and can help the child become a self-regulated learner.[39] Consistently, studies have shown that students who have enthusiastic teachers develop better focus that leads to higher academic performance.[40] Children who enjoy learning "can catch" the spark of enthusiasm from the teacher.[41]

Some dictionaries actually define enthusiasm as a sharing of enjoyment.[42] The teacher enjoys teaching a particular lesson because a student learns something new and enjoys the experience. The student's subsequent delight reinforces the teacher's sense of satisfaction.[43]

With regard to teachers, there exist different kinds of enthusiasm—the first is an enthusiasm for the subject itself.[44] The enthusiastic science teacher plays around with experiments at home for fun, reads the latest news concerning scientific breakthroughs, and loves talking about science. The enthusiastic social studies teacher is constantly reading and writing, happily getting lost in bookstores, visiting historical sites, pondering alternative outcomes of history.

Another kind of enthusiasm has to do with the satisfaction derived from the act of teaching, itself. This second kind of enthusiasm is what most people refer to when they speak of the "non-monetary rewards of teaching."[45] Teachers might not make a lot of money, but they experience the satisfaction of devoting themselves to helping children learn.

A fortunate child is one who has a teacher with both kinds of enthusiasm—a love for their subject and a love for the profession.

You could hire a cameraman to follow your child around all day, record all interactions, and then view, study, and analyze the resulting film at the end of each day. But, that approach is not recommended. The only real way for you to know the truth about your child's life at school is for the teacher to tell you.[46] Such honesty requires an open, positive, reciprocal relationship with the teacher.

You also want the teacher to be able to communicate forthrightly with your child—to offer prompt, insightful feedback whenever possible. Indeed, feedback must be timely and specific to be effective.[47] A student who receives a paper with only bright, red Xs on it a month after the assignment was turned in receives little benefit while a student who receives prompt, constructive feedback may learn a lot—perhaps even more than would have been learned with a perfect score.

Feedback that is focused solely on task performance—is the answer wrong or right?—may be of limited use.[48] Broader feedback, involving comments on processes and metacognition are where the greater learning occurs.[49]

Despite the value of feedback, a teacher receives no extra compensation or recognition for providing it—other than your (and your child's) thanks.

Writing feedback can be time-consuming and is against a teacher's own self-interest because the system, as it exists, encourages facile assignments and the proliferation of gold stars and smiley face stickers.[50]

Yet, honest feedback delivered in a timely and sensitive manner is the essence of learning.[51] As long as a teacher's responses are accurate, sensitive, and genuine, feedback has been proven, again and again, to be incredibly effective.[52]

To understand errors, especially in mathematics and the sciences, students need more information than "Your answer is wrong!" They need to be able to get at their thought processes to identify the source of the misunderstanding. However, trying to delve into how a child thinks involves individualized instruction and much one-on-one conversation.

When someone teaches six classes with an average of thirty students per class in a day, there may be little room for individualization. It may be useful to consider that there exist at least four different kinds of feedback, as shown in figure 11.1.[53]

The sheer volume of papers is the reason that most teachers prefer multiple-choice assignments and exams, even in subjects, such as language arts and social studies, though the writing of short answers and essays are far better ways to assess knowledge, application, and synthesis.[54] Although it is widely recognized by experts in assessment that multiple-choice tests "are not useful for assessing critical or higher order thinking in a subject,"[55] multiple-choice tests and assignments dominate because they are quick to administer and quick to grade.

KIND OF FEEDBACK	TASK PERFORMANCE	THE PROCESS ASSOCIATED WITH PERFORMING THE TASK	THE KIND OF THINKING REQUIRED (METACOGNITION)	PERSONAL OR SELF-RELATED
RELEVANT QUESTIONS	Did the student get the correct answer? How close is the performance to the desired outcome?	What process was used to achieve the result? What would be the optimal process?	How did the student think about solving the problem? What kind of thinking would lend itself to solving such a problem?	How should the performance on this task be viewed in light of the performance on previous tasks and potential?

Figure 11.1 Kinds of Feedback.

A teacher with the aforementioned (typical) 180-student class load who assigns an essay and spends only five minutes reading and grading each essay will have to devote fifteen hours of nonstop work to the task. Because a teacher's time is limited, the natural inclination is to offer assignments that are easy to grade and require no feedback. Such a philosophy saves the teacher time but does not enhance the quality of student learning.

Unfortunately, the current system also encourages teachers to lie.[56] Most schools require that a teacher provide exhaustive documentation for any student who has a chance of earning a failing grade. The typical process involves a teacher filling out numerous forms with all grades, missing assignments, explanations, absences, behavior patterns, and descriptions of all attempts and results of efforts to intervene. Some schools require "failure reports" daily or weekly. For students in special education, the bureaucracy is even deeper and more time-consuming.

In this way, giving low grades obligates a teacher to meet with administrators, counselors, and parents in meetings before or after school. Often, in these kinds of meetings, discussions will drift into examining the teacher's competence. Why has the teacher failed in getting the student to learn? What is the teacher doing wrong?

In a private school, failing grades can result in a student switching schools and a loss of tuition dollars. In public schools, students with failing grades lower a school's ranking, reputation, and possibly its funding. A teacher avoids the pain of excruciating bureaucracy and confrontation if they simply hand out passing scores to all.

By themselves, numbers may mean very little. What does a "63" or a "99" actually represent? A 63 on the written portion of an Advanced Placement Test likely represents higher intellectual development than a 99 on a worksheet in a remedial course, for example.

Thomas Jefferson was right when he wrote to a friend that "honesty is the first chapter in the book of wisdom."[57] Without honesty, little can be accomplished in education.

STORY

A teacher's honesty is essential. A parent cannot make wise decisions on behalf of a child with incorrect information. In what areas does the child excel? In what areas does the child struggle? Do they get along well with peers or are they social pariahs? Do they contribute to class or do they act as saboteurs?

A boy named Eric first learned to play the trumpet in elementary school, and his music teacher always would expound to his parents that Eric was immensely talented, with "natural musical abilities." Yet, when Eric's parents listened to him practice at home and when they attended the school's musical concert, Eric's talent was less apparent. The band's concert performance at school had been discordant and arrhythmic, yet the only words Eric's parents had ever heard from the music teacher had been extremely positive.

The next year, the school hired a new music director, who was demanding and quite precise about areas of improvement. At first, Eric resented the increased workload, but his playing improved markedly as did the quality of the band concerts. The new, highly demanding music director prioritized the band's performance and individual student development over keeping parents happy.

The band improved dramatically and became a "cool" elective at school. Membership in the band grew, their sound improved every year, and they began winning contests.

In his Nobel Prize acceptance speech, Martin Luther King proclaimed that "unarmed truth and unconditional love would have the final word." That particular combination—truth and love—are at the heart of learning.

STRATEGY 11C: CONSIDER THE TEACHER'S EDUCATION AND EXPERIENCE

An obvious way to achieve an adequate and equitable education for every child would be to ensure that only brilliant, enthusiastic, compassionate human beings serve as teachers. In the mid-nineteenth century, states began developing a designation to assure the public of an individual's fitness for the teaching profession. Eventually, all states came to use *certification* as proof of a teacher's proficiency.[58]

The purpose of any certification, be it for practicing law (Juris Doctor), mixing drugs (PharmD), or saving lives as an Emergency Medical Technician (EMT), is to provide an assurance of competence. Individuals incapable of mastering the skills necessary in a particular profession are not certified; rather, they are prohibited from entering the profession.

An incompetent lawyer unable to identify violations of the law puts his/her clients at risk. An incompetent pharmacist can do irreparable harm to a person by issuing the wrong prescription. An incompetent EMT can endanger a patient's life by failing to properly respond to symptoms. An incompetent teacher can harm a child's cognitive, emotional, and social development for life.

For such a highly demanding, delicate, and consequential job, one might expect that the requirements for becoming a teacher might be set exceedingly high, but they are not. In fact, in most states, a person with a bachelor's degree will find it easier to get a certificate in teaching than a certificate in just about any other professional field.

To become a mortician in Ohio, for example, a person must complete a bachelor's degree from an accredited program, plus up to two years of postbaccalaureate study in mortuary science, achieve a passing score on a rigorous exam, and fulfill a one- to two-year internship under the guidance of an established, master mortician.[59] There is no "alternate route" to becoming a mortician in Ohio. The routes to obtaining certification in mortuary science and teaching are compared in figure 11.2.

The check mark denotes a more rigorous requirement; the X denotes an easier requirement. As can be seen readily from the comparison, it is more challenging to qualify as a mortician than to qualify as a teacher in Ohio.

Alternate routes to becoming a teacher in Ohio, as in many states, abound. One alternative path called the American Board for Certification of Teacher Excellence (ABCTE) sells teacher certification online as if it were a commercial product, like a kitchen appliance. Consider the following sales pitch featured on ABCTE's website (https://www.americanboard.org/ohio/):

> You can become a teacher in Ohio on your own schedule, without quitting your current job or going into debt. The program is entirely online, and you can complete it in less than one month. No additional university class time is required and at a total program cost of $900.[60]

According to Ohio law, the State Board of Education is responsible for ensuring the quality of teachers. The Ohio Board of Education is charged to

> formulate and prescribe minimum standards to be applied to all elementary and secondary schools in this state for the purpose of providing children access to a general education of high quality according to the learning needs of each individual, including students with disabilities, economically disadvantaged students, English learners, and students identified as gifted. Such standards shall provide adequately for: the licensing of teachers.[61]

Results on achievement tests have shown that students taught by ABCTE teachers perform much worse than students taught by teachers who were educated in university-based programs.[62]

In many states like Ohio, teacher preparation has moved out of universities and into the hands of corporations.[63] In Texas, for example, more than three in four new teachers now point-and-click their way to certification over the Internet, bypassing university preparation and foregoing student teaching completely.[64] Texas point-and-click programs received F's for the quality of their programs and F's for their clinical experiences because most have neither.[65]

	MORTICIAN	**TEACHER**
EDUCATION	College degree in mortuary science from an accredited program ✓	A degree in any field X
REQUIRED POST-BACCALAUREATE STUDY	Two years of graduate coursework from an accredited program ✓	No additional course work required X
EXAMS	Two-part National Board Examination created by American Board of Funeral Service Educators ✓	Pedagogical and content-area tests created by Pearson Corporation X
EXAM PASS RATES	Pass rate for arts majors=73% Pass rate for science majors=67%[1] ✓	Pass rate for pedagogy=94% Pass rate for content (early childhood)=91%[2] X
INTERNSHIP	One- to two-year internship under guidance of master mortician ✓	No internship required X
ALTERNATIVE ROUTES	None ✓	Plenty of alternative routes X

---

[1] American Board of Funeral Service Educators (2021). *ABFSE Directory*. Woodbury Heights, New Jersey: ABFSE. https://www.abfse.org/docs/ABFSEDirectory.pdf. Data for Ohio begins on p. 51.

[2] Ohio Department of Education (2021). *Ohio educator licensure examination pass rates*. Columbus, Ohio: Ohio Department of Education. https://miamioh.edu/ehs/about/educator-prep-data/oae-pass-rates/index.html

Figure 11.2 Pathways to Becoming a Mortician versus Becoming a Teacher in Ohio.

Over the past thirty years, shoddy online graduate programs in education have proliferated, so a parent must make sure that a teacher's degree is from a respectable institution and not from a "cheap and quick" diploma mill.[66] If a teacher lists no student teaching experience on a resume, for example, it probably means that they had none.[67]

A report from the National Conference of State Legislatures notes, "Most state education systems are falling dangerously behind the world. . . . At this pace, we will struggle to compete economically against even developing nations, and our children will struggle to find jobs in the global economy."[68]

Unfortunately, as numerous studies have pointed out, the worst teachers tend to congregate in the most troubled schools.[69]

Horace Mann writes:

> Our means of education are the grand machinery by which the "raw material" of human nature can be worked up into inventors and discoverers, into skilled artisans and scientific farmers, into scholars and jurists, into the founders of benevolent institutions, and the great expounders of ethical and theological science.[70]

The data is irrefutable: the quality of the teacher matters.[71] A teacher who has the education and experience to help your child identify their talents and realize their potential is invaluable. "Teachers matter more to student achievement than any other aspect of schooling."[72]

Ten desirable characteristics for a teacher are as follows:

1. Cares for your child
2. Enjoys working with children
3. Has previous teaching experience, including student teaching
4. Is certified to teach the subject matter
5. Is certified to teach at your child's grade level
6. Attended a real university
7. Is smart
8. Is honest
9. Is enthusiastic
10. Is active, yet accessible

STORY

In Texas, one result of the slipshod approach to teacher preparation has been the meteoric rise of teacher misconduct. Thousands of cases of teacher misconduct, typically involving some sort of sexual impropriety, have occurred since Texas allowed prospective teachers to purchase certification online rather than take a university-based program of study.[73] The Texas Education Agency has been put in the awkward position of continually asking its legislature for money to investigate the thousands of new and backlogged allegations of teacher misconduct.[74]

The organization simply cannot keep up with the burgeoning number of infractions from non-vetted teachers.[75] In a case that the TEA did investigate, a teacher at a Texas charter school was found guilty of molesting young boys and was sentenced to prison.[76]

A second outcome for Texas has been a consistent decline in student achievement. Test scores of African American and Hispanic students in Texas on the Scholastic Aptitude Test (SAT), in particular, have steadily declined and now are among the lowest in the nation. The College Board estimates that only 14 percent of African American students and 19 percent of Hispanic students in Texas are now "college ready."[77]

Strategy 12

Get into Gifted

Finding the right school is only one piece of the puzzle. Once you have decided on a school and your child has been admitted (easy in public schools, more challenging in private schools), the next step is deciding on the right course of study. While the inclination might be to take easy courses at least every once in a while, the research overwhelmingly supports the idea that demanding courses yield the most consistently beneficial results.[1]

A recent study of the effects of taking advanced courses found that "even taking just one advanced course improves students' test scores, likelihood of graduating from high school, and likelihood of attending a four-year university."[2]

A course of study has implications beyond the theoretical, as students can accumulate a semester or several semesters worth of college credit by taking and passing AP courses. Making good grades on AP exams and scoring high on standardized tests, such as the SAT and the American College Testing (ACT), increases options for college and can decrease college costs.

To be blunt—gifted education in the United States is an unorganized mess. The federal government does not support gifted education,[3] other than through the Jacob K. Javits Gifted and Talented Students Education Act, which offers small grants for identifying and providing services to gifted minority students, English language learners, and children with disabilities.[4]

At the state level, the highest funding for gifted education in the United States is only about $80 per pupil, provided to students who live in Iowa. West Virginia only spends .03 (three cents) on gifted education per pupil. Before criticizing West Virginia, it should be known that many states contribute absolutely nothing to gifted education. So, West Virginia's contribution of three cents to gifted education is, at least, three cents more than many states spend.

When considering that total expenditures on public education exceed 800 billion dollars per year, one might suppose there could be at least a little room for improving the funding for the education of America's brightest children.[5] Yet, federal funding earmarked specifically for gifted education is almost nonexistent.[6] Nationwide, relatively few students are enrolled in courses designed for the academically gifted—only 6 percent.

Despite the lack of financial support, gifted education is undisputedly the most desirable destination for students, as elucidated below.

TRACKING

Almost all schools employ tracking, the process of grouping students together by ability, even if a school tries to claim otherwise.[7] Usually by sixth or seventh grade, three tracks become evident—honors, regular, and remedial—though sometimes the tracks are named so that it is difficult for an outsider to discern the real academic level of a course. Rest assured, however, that students are well aware of the differences.

An English course entitled "Advanced Communications," in actuality might be a remedial reading course for students who had flunked English the year before. Courses with "basic," "applied," "practical," "general," or "fundamentals" in their title, such as "Applied Biology" or "Math Fundamentals" often designate the lowest tier among courses.[8]

Larger high schools may employ an additional track for the gifted and talented or students enrolled in AP or International Baccalaureate (IB) courses. So, the highest level becomes AP or IB. Some universities and colleges offer credit for passing scores on AP/IB exams and students in high school increasingly have the chance to take courses for college credit while they are "simultaneously" enrolled in high school. When a school offers AP/IB classes, it usually means that courses with *honors* in front of their title, that is, *Honors English, Honors Biology* inhabit a second tier, a less rigorous option.

In a school that offers AP/IB classes, enrolling in honors classes usually means that a student could not handle the work of AP/IB classes or that their work life or home life prevented them from taking the time-consuming courses associated with AP/IB.

The rule for course selection is, "Always take the highest possible level of course, even if it may not be an area of strength for your child." If your child does not qualify for advanced courses, challenge the criteria for selection. No fixed standard for determining who is gifted and who is not gifted has been established by the National Association for Gifted Children (NAGC). Indeed, the opening sentence in NAGC's multipage definition of giftedness is as follows:

> NAGC believes it is essential to define giftedness in a way that both reflects best thinking in the field and moves beyond a focus on identification criteria to a deeper understanding of the complex nature of giftedness and the multifaceted approach to services required to appropriately serve students with gifts and talents.[9]

Many of the longitudinal studies of giftedness confirm that brilliance may not show up in standardized tests. In studies of giftedness in the early twentieth century, researcher Lewis Terman wanted to determine if a gifted child's superior test scores might lead to greater accomplishments later in life.[10] Terman found that some students he rejected for his study as being "not smart enough" turned out to do quite well. Among Terman's rejected children were future Nobel Prize Winners, celebrated inventors and scientists, famous poets, writers, and billionaires.[11]

If your child does not qualify for the gifted program according to a school's particular set of standards, as a parent, you have the right to plead the case that your child may fall under the *complex, multifaceted* part of NAGC's definition of giftedness. You can always mention the Terman studies and the difficulty of accurately assessing giftedness. The truth is that "greater talent in one pupil may be equalled by extra effort in another."[12]

To reiterate, there are no accepted criteria for giftedness, and genius is usually determined only after the fact. That is, it is only after the Nobel, Pulitzer, Booker, and Breakthrough Prizes have been awarded that people say, "Obviously, he/she was gifted."

Perhaps the best reason for having your child take the most difficult classes is that it puts them into regular contact with students who might really want to learn. In regular or remedial classes, the focus may be on other goals, often the attainment of the highest possible grade with the least possible effort.[13] As a result, a teacher of regular or remedial classes often spends more time and effort on trying to manage student behavior and adapting curriculum for special needs than on teaching lessons.[14]

When a teacher alerts an AP/IB student that his/her grade is falling, it will likely induce anxiety and elicit motivation to improve. The norm in an advanced class is to desire academic success. Concern for grades is less evident among students in regular or remedial courses.[15]

A second benefit of more academically challenging classes is that they are usually taught by more experienced teachers.[16] An AP/IB course is typically inhabited by students who are motivated to learn, so these courses tend to attract teachers who are also actively engaged with a particular subject.[17] In addition, teachers who teach AP/IB may be required to take intensive, additional academic preparation, which keeps them up-to-date and savvy about recent changes in the field.[18]

To summarize, five compelling reasons for getting your children into gifted classes are as follows:

1. Less time is spent on correcting misbehaviors during class
2. Courses are more intellectually demanding
3. There is greater opportunity to learn from very bright peers
4. Gifted courses are typically taught by a school's best teachers
5. Students can get college credit for gifted courses taken in high school

TESTING

While the American obsession with testing is regrettable, it is also true that a high standardized test score wields great power. Standardized tests deserve no love, but a smart parent knows to allot them at least a modicum of respect.

Once upon a time, standardized tests were used by schools chiefly as diagnostic tools, not as mechanisms with which to rank and rate.[19] As diagnostic tools, standardized tests can help uncover untapped ability and help identify academic areas of weakness. One of my colleagues, who was an expert in assessment, was fond of saying "High test scores might reveal talent, but low test scores reveal nothing."

Unfortunately, the concept of the test as supplementary to school performance has been turned on its head over the past forty years.[20] Now a high score on the SAT or the ACT can supersede an impeccable record of accomplishment hard-won over twelve years of formal K–12 schooling and countless hours of altruistic, volunteer work.[21]

While test scores mean nothing in themselves, if your child is capable of scoring highly, understand that a high score could translate into considerably reduced tuition costs. Some institutions of higher education have stopped using test scores as the *primary* criterion for an admissions decision, yet even these institutions still consider a test score as *part of the array* of considerations.[22]

In other words, even at institutions that claim to no longer require standardized tests, scores on standardized tests still can have influence. Standardized tests are biased and they may not indicate much about academic potential, but in the real world of college admissions, they pack a wallop.[23]

STORY

Currently, many of the most prestigious institutions of higher education calculate potential academic scholarship awards based upon an applicants' test scores and not much else. A student named Hollis, a child with two professors for parents, applied and was accepted into a prominent, Ivy League university. When Hollis was in high school, she made high grades in AP classes and was a member of a state championship athletic team.

When Hollis took the ACT exam, she scored a 31, sufficiently high to get her admitted into most colleges and universities. She wanted to retake the ACT to increase her score to give her even more options, but her parents discouraged her, emphasizing that a test score was a trivial matter.

She had fulfilled the obligation of taking a test in order to get admitted into an institution of higher education and that was enough. She need not expend any more effort trying to ramp up a test score simply to impress others.

Any expert in assessment will readily admit that a few points on a standardized test is neither meaningful nor significant.[24] So, while the parents were technically correct about the inconsequential nature of a few, silly points on the ACT, the advice turned out to be costly. Only after Hollis enrolled was it discovered that if she had retaken the ACT and scored only one point higher, the university would have increased the amount of her scholarship by $10,000 per year.

In other words, the parent's anti-test-taking advice tacked an additional $40,000 onto the cost of Hollis's university education.

Strategy 13

Encourage Participation in Noncontact Sports; No Team Sports Before Age Ten

Some parents may consider school sports overly time-consuming or irrelevant, but the benefits of participation in sports for teens are substantial.[1] For some students, sports might serve as the sole bright spot in a day at school.[2]

Participation in sports for teens is associated with "better educational outcomes, enhanced school engagement, positive life skills, and healthier behaviors." Nationwide, more than half of all high school students in America, over ten million children, participate in sports.[3]

There is little room for alcohol, drugs, or off-task behavior when an adolescent on a cross-country team is expected to run 50 miles or more over the course of a week or when a swimmer must move her/his body through the water for several miles before school every morning.[4]

However, a common mistake that many parents make is starting children in team sports too early, when neither the child's body nor mind is ready. The American Academy of Pediatrics (AAP) notes that before age ten, children may not possess "the hand-eye coordination needed to perform complex motor skills" and may also lack the maturity to be able to focus on team goals or strategies.[5]

From ages ten to twelve, a child's maturity improves significantly, but the AAP still suggests that the primary goal of participation in sports at this age should be on "skill development, fun, and participation, not competition."[6] So, for many children, the earliest participation in team sports might begin around age thirteen.

Undoubtedly, the impulse to join a team can be strong.[7] Joining a team can be attractive for a teen because teams offer an instantaneous opportunity to belong to a peer group.[8] Once a teen is a member of a team, his/her identity is merged, at least somewhat, with the team's.[9] Chances are, they can find at least one person associated with the team to sit with during lunch at school.

Four benefits associated with teens participating in sports are as follows:

1. Students who participate in sports tend to have higher academic achievement (than students who do not participate in sports)[10]
2. Students who participate in sports tend to have a lower incidence of mental health problems[11]
3. Students who participate in sports tend to have better overall physical health[12]
4. Students who participate in sports tend to have higher levels of self-esteem[13]

Track and field, cross-country, tennis, golf, swimming, and diving are the safest school sports, followed by softball/baseball and volleyball. Contact sports, such as football, ice hockey, lacrosse, wrestling, and soccer have higher risks of injury. Basketball and cheerleading are in the middle zone. Helping children choose a suitable sport can be tricky, especially if peers are involved.

Sorting fact from fiction about possible dangers of participating in sports can be confusing. One study might claim that cheerleading is the most dangerous sport,[14] while another might claim it is one of the safest[15] (as noted above, cheerleading is actually in the middle zone). In general, articles from the AAP, American Medical Association, and refereed journals, such as *The Journal of Athletic Training*, are trustworthy.

Many children gravitate to contact sports and sometimes it is difficult, if not impossible, to dissuade them from participation. About a half million boys get injured playing high school football in an average year, with many of the injuries involving concussion.[16] Sports-related concussion is a form of traumatic brain injury that can cause severe, possibly lasting, "physical, emotional, and cognitive" damage.[17]

Although most children who experience traumatic brain injury recover, "10-40% develop chronic post-concussive symptoms."[18] Potentially negative outcomes include increased risk of amyotrophic lateral sclerosis (a breaking down of nerves in the brain), Alzheimer's disease, Parkinson's disease, and dementia.[19]

There are many ways to assess the relative safety of a sport, but most parents would agree that the prospect of a concussion is more threatening than a sprained ankle or a sore shoulder. A sprained ankle or sore shoulder can heal over time and has no potential impact on cognitive functioning.

One of the worst outcomes of repeated concussions is the possible development of chronic traumatic encephalopathy (CTE), a neurodegenerative disease that can lead to "dramatic changes in mood, behavior, and cognition, frequently resulting in debilitating dementia."[20]

In a well-known study of the brains of deceased high school, collegiate, and professional football players, it was found that 87 percent of all football players had CTE.[21] When examining the brains of professional football players exclusively, "110 of 111 former National Football league players (99%)" were found to have CTE.[22]

Figures 13.1, 13.2, and 13.3 represent rates of concussion by sport. Concussion while participating in track and field, tennis, or golf is relatively rare, so these sports earn a rating of 1, which designates "low risk."[23] The rates of concussion in other sports is calculated in relation to this "low risk" rate of 1.

SPORT	MEAN RATE OF INJURY	PROBABILITY OF INJURY COMPARED TO TRACK	COMMENTS[i]
TRACK, TENNIS, GOLF (BOYS & GIRLS) 	.2	1	Low incidence of concussions. "Track events most commonly associated with concussions were pole vaulting and high jump"
SWIMMING, DIVING (BOYS & GIRLS) 	.3	1.5	Low incidence of concussions. "Concussion most commonly resulted from contact with the deck"
BOYS'  BASEBALL	.8	4	Low incidence of concussions. "A greater proportion of baseball players' concussions resulted from being hit by a pitch than did softball players' concussions"[ii]

---

[i] Except where noted, citations for figures 14a, 14b, and 14c are from: Marar, M., McIlvain, N., Fields, S., & Dawn, R. (2012). Epidemiology of concussions among United States high school athletes in 20 sports. *The American Journal of Sports Medicine* 40(4), 747-755.

[ii] Comstock, R.D.; & Pierpoint, L. (2019). *Summary report: National high school sports-related injury surveillance study, 2018-2019 school year.* Aurora, Colorado: Colorado School of Public Health. https://coloradosph.cuanschutz.edu/docs/librariesprovider204/default-document-library/2018-19.pdf?sfvrsn=d26400b9_2.

Figure 13.1   Rates of Concussion by Sport, Low Risk.

SPORT	MEAN RATE OF INJURY	PROBABILITY OF INJURY COMPARED TO TRACK	COMMENTS[i]
GIRLS' VOLLEYBALL 	1.9	10	Low incidence of concussions. "About half of concussions were sustained by outside hitter and setter positions"
GIRLS' SOFTBALL 	2	10	"Baseball and softball players sustained over a quarter of concussions as a result of fielding a batted ball"
BOYS' BASKETBALL 	2.1	11	"A larger proportion of boys than girls sustained a concussion due to play-player contact"
CHEERLEADING 	2.4	12	"The activity associated with 90.9% of concussions was a stunt"
GIRLS' FIELD HOCKEY 	2.5	13	"Player-equipment contact (ball or stick) resulted in 60.8% of concussions"
BOYS' SOCCER 	2.8	14	"The activity most frequently associated with concussion was heading the ball"[ii]

[i] Except where noted, citations for figures 14a, 14b, and 14c are from: Marar, M., McIlvain, N., Fields, S., & Dawn, R. (2012). Epidemiology of concussions among United States high school athletes in 20 sports. *The American Journal of Sports Medicine* 40(4), 747-755.

[ii] Rechel, J.; Yard, E.; Comstock, R. D. (2012). An epidemiologic comparison of high school sports injuries sustained in practice and competition. *Journal of Athletic Training* 43(2), 197-204.

Figure 13.2 Rates of Concussion by Sport, Middle Risk.

Football gets a rating of 42, meaning that the probability of a boy experiencing a concussion while participating in football is 42 times greater than the likelihood of a boy experiencing a concussion while participating in track

SPORT	MEAN RATE OF INJURY[i]	PROBABILITY OF INJURY COMPARED TO TRACK	COMMENTS[ii]
FOOTBALL	8.4	42	"Tackling and being tackled were responsible for 62.5% of concussions"
BOYS' ICE HOCKEY	6.6	33	"Concussions represented a greater proportion of total injuries...than all other sports studied"
GIRLS' SOCCER	5.8	29	"Girls had a higher rate of concussion than boys"
LACROSSE BOYS/GIRLS	4.5/3.9	23/18	BOYS-"Concussion most commonly resulted from player-player contact (76.7%)" GIRLS-"Among all girls' sports studied, concussions represented a greater proportion of total injuries"
GIRLS' BASKETBALL	3.5	18	"Among girls, a greater proportion of concussions were sustained while defending"
BOYS' WRESTLING	3.5	18	"An activity most commonly associated with concussion was takedowns (58.7% of concussions)"

[i] Average rates of concussion were calculated by averaging concussion rates in two studies: Comstock, R.D.; & Pierpoint, L. (2019). *Summary report: National high school sports-related injury surveillance study, 2018-2019 school year*. Aurora, Colorado: Colorado School of Public Health. https://coloradosph.cuanschutz.edu/docs/librariesprovider204/default-document-library/2018-19.pdf?sfvrsn=d26400b9_2 and Rechel, J.; Yard, E.; Comstock, R. D. (2012). An epidemiologic comparison of high school sports injuries sustained in practice and competition. *Journal of Athletic Training* 43(2), 197-204. Golf and tennis have low rates of concussion and thus, are grouped with track and field, which has the lowest rates of concussion among sports on which data is collected.

[ii] Except where noted, citations for figures 14a, 14b, and 14c are from: Marar, M., McIlvain, N., Fields, S., & Dawn, R. (2012). Epidemiology of concussions among United States high school athletes in 20 sports. *The American Journal of Sports Medicine* 40(4), 747-755.

Figure 13.3   Rates of Concussion by Sport, High Risk.

or tennis (each of which has a rating of 1). The probability of a girl getting a concussion by participating in soccer is 29 times greater than the probability of a girl getting a concussion in swimming or golf. The far-right column, "key comments" offers insights about specific sports from recent studies of concussion in sports.

It is useful to be aware that children who play contact sports have a significantly greater chance of injury than if they played noncontact sports. It is also useful to be aware that few players who participate in high-injury sports, such as football or ice hockey, play those sports past the age of eighteen. On the other hand, running, swimming, tennis, and golf can be lifelong activities.

Getting a scholarship to play sports in college is another way to reduce college costs. Although millions of students participate in high school sports, only about 2 percent ever receive a scholarship offer to play sports in college.[24] From that tiny group, even fewer individuals are able to make the transition from amateur to professional sports.[25] Researchers at Georgia State University estimate that the chances of a high school athlete becoming a professional athlete at about 1 in 16,000.[26]

STORY

As with a teacher, an ethos of care should take precedence over other attributes when considering the right coach. Most former players of school sports are able to recount in glorious detail countless instances of maltreatment by unruly and win-at-all-costs coaches. Common abuse includes encouraging players to stay in a game when injured; screaming demeaning insults; physically threatening players, opponents, parents, and referees; and basically, doing anything at all in order to come out on top at the end of a game.

The "age 10 rule" dictates that no child under ten years of age should join any sports team. At baseball games, for example, most young children under ten will spend more time digging holes in the outfield and examining the ants in the grass than actually watching what might be transpiring in the game. Practices and games for children under age ten tend to be a waste of time, especially for the child.

Strategy 14

Take Advantage of School Services

School staff can be of immeasurable help, but you have to

1. know they exist
2. know what they offer
3. know how to utilize them intelligently

All schools have a dizzying array of staff, many of whom most people never meet—cafeteria servers, disability specialists, teacher aides, in-school suspension instructors, translators, social workers, receptionists, clerks, assistant principals, security guards, coaches, counselors, nurses, librarians, and language pathologists.

In large schools, it can be particularly daunting to try to become acquainted with all the moving parts, but the effort to learn names and phone numbers and to connect directly with staff is well worth it. Otherwise, the only connection you will ever have to school staff will be a disembodied voice on the school's (likely insipid) prerecorded phone message. Life in a school is continually busy. If you do not ask, you will not receive.

School services are not important until your child gets sick, wants to read a book, has a personal problem, experiences difficulty with learning, or decides that he/she needs a job or wants to go to college. During times of financial stress, schools tend to cut expenses that are not directly related to classroom instruction, which usually translates into a reduction or elimination of nurses, librarians, and counselors, a grievous sin.[1]

A significant problem with reducing support staff is that they rarely, if ever, are returned to full strength. Because physical health, mental health, reading, and thinking are essential for a child's development, consider schools whose staff includes qualified nurses, counselors, and librarians. This is not as easy as it sounds.

SCHOOL NURSES

Having a nurse on-site at a school would seem an essential service, but most schools in the United States have no full-time nurse.[2] Hawaiian public schools employ no nurses at all and, in Utah, there are around 5,000 students for every nurse.[3] Public schools in the Northeast tend to have the best student-to-nurse ratios. School nurses are most prevalent in Vermont, where the student-to-nurse ratio is the lowest in the country, 270:1. Most private schools and many charter schools employ no school nurse.[4]

Here's a startling fact that should substantiate the importance of every school having at least one full-time nurse on staff: Students are more than twenty times more likely to visit a nurse at school for health-related issues than a doctor or nurse outside of school.[5]

During volatile times, such as the COVID-19 pandemic, having a school nurse at school would offer some assurance for both parents and students. A school nurse is particularly useful if your child happens to have asthma, a food allergy, occasional problems with anxiety, takes medication, or becomes sick while at school. Four essential services provided by a school nurse are as follows:

1. A school nurse assesses health complaints, administers medication, and cares for students with specific health care needs
2. A school nurse establishes and implements responses to emergencies
3. A school nurse initiates screenings, verifies immunizations, and reports on student health
4. A school nurse identifies and manages students' chronic health care needs

A good school nurse can diagnose symptoms, move a sick child from the classroom to the school clinic, provide emergency care, and quickly notify a parent—all in a matter of minutes. Without a good nurse, there is no help when a child becomes ill.

SCHOOL LIBRARIANS

As with school nurses, the number of credentialed, full-time librarians in public schools keeps dwindling. While the number of students has risen in

K–12 schools in recent years, the number of librarians has proportionally decreased.[6]

According to the American Association of School Librarians, there should be at least one full-time, certified librarian in every school,[7] but most schools do not employ full-time, certified librarians.[8] In California, only 9 percent of public school libraries are managed by a certified librarian—this 9 percent includes part-time employees and untrained assistants.[9]

Nationally, there are, on average, 1,200 students for every librarian, including uncertified and part-time librarians, though the ratio of students to librarians is much higher in many schools.[10] Most charter schools do not have libraries, so they employ no librarians.[11]

Yet, the quality of the school library and the quality of the school librarian can be a boon for student achievement.[12] The COVID-19 crisis also brought to light the decline of school libraries/media centers and the dearth of certified librarians.[13] During COVID-19, the few schools that had certified librarians and media specialists on staff were more prepared to transfer instruction to an online format when circumstances forced school buildings to close.[14]

Schools without certified librarians and media specialists had no one to lead online initiatives or help with technology questions, thus efforts at these schools tended to be ineffective and inconsistent.[15] Four key contributions made by librarians include the following.

1. A school librarian makes access easy to information in a wide variety of formats
2. A school librarian instructs students and teachers how to acquire, evaluate, and use information
3. A school librarian introduces children and young adults to books, journals, online resources, and new technologies
4. A school librarian helps students learn how to do research

When school buildings are open, a library run by a certified librarian can dramatically enrich the quality of learning for the entire student body.[16] Numerous studies of school libraries have confirmed that a "school library with appropriate staffing, adequate funding, and a rich collection of materials in various formats makes a positive impact on literacy as well as on overall academic achievement."[17]

Smart parents understand that a modern, welcoming, well-stocked library on campus where students are welcome to hang out, read, and work before, during, and after school is of immense value.

COUNSELORS

For most of the twentieth century, the job of a school counselor was to help identify student strengths and weaknesses, to provide psychological services, to be available when a student needed someone to talk to and, in high school, to help students prepare for the world of work or higher education.[18] One of the unintended consequences of the national movement toward assessment was to repurpose school counselors as "data managers" for testing and evaluation. Indeed, counselors report that they routinely spend more time in activities, such as testing, creating class schedules, or writing reports, than interacting with students.[19]

An effective counselor is accessible, influential, and all-too-rare. The Center for Disease Control and Prevention estimates that one in five children has a diagnosable mental disorder[20] and "depression, anxiety, and behavioral/conduct problems are prevalent among U.S. children and adolescents."[21]

In addition to helping a child get through a "terrible, horrible, no good, very bad day,"[22] a counselor can help a parent circumvent bad teachers and get a child into gifted classes, even with poor test results. A high school counselor can offer an inside track to jobs, college applications, and how to secure money to pay for college.

While the American School Counselor Association[23] recommends a ratio of at least one counselor for every 250 students,[24] less than 10 percent of counselors actually have such a light load.[25] Most counselors serve hundreds of students; some counselors serve thousands.[26]

Studies have shown that an effective counselor can positively impact a child's mental health, study skills, attendance rate, achievement, acceptance into college, and the amount of financial aid a student is offered.[27]

When visiting a school, make sure to visit with the counselor. Does the counselor actually engage with students on a one-to-one basis concerning academics, personal problems, or future plans? The ratio of students to counselors is about the same in public and private schools. However, because there is less poverty in private schools, private school counselors tend to spend more time talking to college admissions staff and less time talking about potential jobs.[28] A good counselor is one who will keep an eye out for your child, not a counselor whose priorities are schedules, tests, and "non-guidance activities."[29]

STORY

Mazie was a brilliant, creative student as an adolescent, but her father was unemployed and often absent, and he refused to file income tax. As a high-achieving student in high school, Mazie would have been eligible to attend college for free on any number of scholarships, but she never learned about such opportunities because the counselor never told her about them.

If Mazie would have had an effective counselor at her school, she could have gone to almost any college in the country for free. As it was, she took a full-time job as a waitress at local International House of Pancakes, attended college part-time, and paid for tuition and books herself. It took Mazie hundreds of late nights at IHOP, six-and-a-half years, and many sleepless nights to earn her bachelor's degree.

Mazie's quest for a college degree was unnecessarily grueling, and she almost didn't make it. Her life could have been quite different if she would have had a counselor who recognized her immense talent and helped her navigate the complexities of applying for college.

Strategy 15

Attend School Events

Most parents lead busy lives, trying to become all that they can be intellectually, socially, and financially, so the prospect of spending hours at a school's open house, speaking to strangers, may seem like an imposition.

Bringing five dozen freshly baked chocolate chip cookies to a rowdy, second-grade classroom on a Wednesday afternoon might seem an incredible inconvenience and a potential time-suck.

Hanging out on Saturdays for hours to watch softball games, selling tickets in a hot, cramped, wooden box for a band concert, participating in tedious Parent-Teacher Association meetings—none of these activities has inherent appeal.

Undeniably, school activities do not satisfy in the way that a $100,000 increase in salary or a first-place finish in a 5K race might satisfy. But school activities are not about you. They are about your child. The time you spend engaged in school activities serves as tangible evidence of your commitment of care.[1]

The research supporting the positive effects of parental involvement at school on a child's life is overwhelming.[2] This does not mean that you have to become a Tiger Mom or Helicopter Dad, but any form of parental involvement beats no involvement[3] and in terms of student outcomes, overparenting is far preferable to neglect.[4]

Predictably, researchers who investigate the effects of parental involvement on children find that children "whose parents are more involved at their child's school, throughout more frequent communication with their child's teacher and other parents, volunteering in school and attending school events, have better school achievement."[5] In addition to higher grades, parental involvement also translates into better social skills for children.[6]

Childhood passes by quickly and the window of opportunity for "being there" for a child is limited. Parents should be prepared for the mundane, but may be surprised and astounded, from time-to-time, by the sublime. Research on the effects of high parental involvement in school events has established five strong associations in children.[7]

1. High parental involvement is positively associated with academic achievement
2. High parental involvement is positively associated with a sense of well-being
3. High parental involvement is positively associated with high attendance
4. High parental involvement is positively associated with optimism
5. High parental involvement is positively associated with high aspirations

High parental involvement means not only direct participation in school events but also helping children with school assignments at home.[8] Researchers have found that the challenge of establishing a dialogue with the child on school matters tends to fall, inevitably and unfairly, on moms. A mother's "involvement in communication with the child on school matters clearly significantly boosts the academic performance of the child, especially on language and information processing."[9]

A father's active interest in a child's life at school has been shown to increase confidence, while also fostering mental dexterity, empathy, and self-control.[10]

On the other hand, a parent's nonparticipation may be harmful in myriad ways.[11] Ideally, participation in school functions should be shared by the entire family.

It is highly likely that at every school event, an administrator also will be in attendance. Two things every parent needs to know about a school administrator are:

1. They hold the power
2. They have continual, complicated, and demanding responsibilities

If your child has a weak teacher, then the request for changing teachers may begin with the school counselor, but the principal always has the last word in such matters. A counselor may resist changing teachers for a variety of reasons, such as the expanding class sizes of good teachers and the diminishing class sizes of bad teachers, but the counselor must abide by the preferences of the principal. Thus, having a positive relationship with the principal is critical, but it also means not trying to schedule meetings about trivial matters.

Principals, public or private, are the "face" of the school and the primary point of contact for anyone who might have a complaint to lodge about anything, from an insensitive football coach to the quality of cafeteria food. Typically, the principal of a school is responsible for all personnel who can be found within the confines of a campus—teachers, librarians, cafeteria workers, coaches, maintenance workers, counselors, and more.

Principals also serve as the main contact for local and state officials. A principal of a public school answers to a district's superintendent, who, in turn, answers to a school board. While private school principals, sometimes called "headmasters," do not have to answer directly to a state department of education, they still must answer to the private school's trustees or board of directors.[12]

The paradox of any administrator's job is that while hired to foster student success and create a nurturing learning environment, they often must spend much of their time engaged in matters unconnected to students in any way.[13]

A typical position description for a principal can fill twenty pages or more.[14] The top eight complaints of principals may provide insight into the nature of their difficult jobs.[15]

1. Insufficient time to get the work done
2. Constant interruptions
3. Volume of paperwork
4. Keeping up with email and other communications
5. Loss of personal time
6. Less money with which to work
7. Teacher evaluations
8. Feeling overwhelmed by job demands

Principals are very much bound by a school's organizational structure and will want to know that you have gone through the appropriate "chain of command" before they speak with you. For example, if your child has had been accused of severe misbehavior, the principal will want to know that you consulted the teacher, counselor, and other employees associated with disciplinary problems first.

In most schools, the person in charge of discipline is an assistant principal (or assistant headmaster), not the principal. This designated person manages the vast majority of behavioral infractions. From the first day of school, good administrators already know the students most likely to have difficulties as well as why they may be trouble-prone. In larger schools, an assistant principal of discipline may be assigned by grade level.

In interactions with school administrators, it helps if a parent is the "positive kind," meaning not the "problem parent." Begin conversations with any administrator gently, saying something along the lines of, "This situation is not working out for my child." Beginning a conversation with an accusation, such as "My child's third grade teacher is an imbecile" or "Your school is crap" is not recommended.

Positive outcomes are possible if a parent has cultivated a good relationship with a principal; not-so-positive outcomes are likely if the parent/principal relationship is sour.

STORY

Teachers readily acknowledge that the parents who attend school "open house" events tend to be the parents that they do not need to see. In other words, it is only the parents of the high-achieving and well-behaved students who come to open house; the parents of low-achieving and poorly behaved students rarely show up.

The pattern remains the same for all school events—sporting events, musical performances, theater, science fair, spelling bee, art shows—the parents of highly accomplished students attend, the parents of struggling or apathetic students stay home. There are many possible reasons for parental noninvolvement, including having to serve as caretaker to other children, conflicting work hours, transportation problems, and other challenges.[16]

One of the very few exceptions to the rule that only the parents of "the good kids" show up at school events from my years as a teacher was David, a surly, combative student, who was always in trouble. At the beginning of the year, David's grades wavered between D and F, he was constantly argumentative, and he had few friends. However, at every open house, at every basketball game and track meet (sports in which David participated), his mom, along with her four younger brothers and sisters, would attend.

Eventually, the counselor discovered that David's father was in prison for peddling methamphetamines and cocaine and that his mother worked a variety of odd jobs to make ends meet. The reason that his mother always brought David and the rest of her children to school functions is that she could not afford to pay a babysitter. David always remained on the rambunctious side, but over time, he improved his grades, became less obnoxious, and gained a few friends. The transformation of David from incorrigible to almost tolerable student was due to the determination of his mother and the presence of his family at school events.

Woody Allen said that "Showing up is 80% of life."[17] With regard to a parent's involvement with a child's education, perhaps the percentage should be higher. Everything beneficial for a child's education starts with the parent showing up.

Notes

PREFACE

1. Oxford English Dictionary (2020). Entry for *education*. https://www.oed.com/view/Entry/59584?redirectedFrom=education#eid.

INTRODUCTION

1. Richer, A., & Binkley, C. (2019, March 12). TV stars and coaches charged in college bribery scheme. *Associated Press News*. https://apnews.com/article/2450688f9e67435c8590e59a1b0e5b47

2. Golden, D., & Burke, D. (2019, October 8). The unseen student victims of the "varsity blues" college-admission scandal. *New Yorker*. https://www.newyorker.com/books/page-turner/the-unseen-student-victims-of-the-varsity-blues-college-admissions-scandal

3. Ingraham, C. (2015, September 14). This chart shows how much more Ivy League grads make than you. *Washington Post*. https://www.washingtonpost.com/news/wonk/wp/2015/09/14/this-chart-shows-why-parents-push-their-kids-so-hard-to-get-into-ivy-league-schools/

4. Bureau of Labor Statistics (2020). *Occupational outlook handbook*. Washington, DC: Government Printing Office. https://www.bls.gov/ooh/

5. Bureau of Labor Statistics (2020, May). *Learn more, earn more: Education leads to higher wages, lower unemployment*. Washington, DC: BLS. https://www.bls.gov/careeroutlook/2020/data-on-display/education-pays.htm

6. World Economic Forum (2020). *The future of jobs report 2020*. Cologny, Switzerland: WEF. http://www3.weforum.org/docs/WEF_Future_of_Jobs_2020.pdf

7. Brewlow, J. (2012, September 21). *By the numbers: Dropping out of high school*. Boston, MA: Frontline. https://www.pbs.org/wgbh/frontline/article/by-the-numbers-dropping-out-of-high-school/

8. Partnership for 21st Century Skills (2009). *P21 framework descriptions.* https://files.eric.ed.gov/fulltext/ED519462.pdf

9. Futrelle, D. (2021). Here's how money really can buy you happiness. *Time.* https://time.com/collection/guide-to-happiness/4856954/can-money-buy-you-happiness/

10. Data based on Twenge, J. M., & Cooper, A. B. (2020). The expanding class divide in happiness in the United States, 1972–2016. *Emotion.* Advance online publication. https://psycnet.apa.org/record/2020-43605-001

11. Twenge, J. M., & Cooper, A. B. (2020). The expanding class divide in happiness in the United States, 1972–2016. *Emotion.* Advance online publication. https://psycnet.apa.org/record/2020-43605-001

12. Kahneman, D., & Deaton, A. (2010, September 21). High income improves evaluation of life but not emotional well-being. *PNAS 107* (38), 16489–16493. https://www.pnas.org/content/107/38/16489

13. Deaton, A., cited in Robison, J. (2011, November 17). Happiness is Love—and $75,000. *Gallup Business Journal.* https://news.gallup.com/businessjournal/150671/happiness-is-love-and-75k.aspx

14. Inflation Calculator (2021). *$75,000 in 2010 is worth $89,589.60 today.* https://www.in2013dollars.com/us/inflation/2010?amount=75000

15. Killingsworth, M. (2021). Experienced well-being rises with income, even above $75,000 per year. *PNAS 118*(4). https://www.pnas.org/content/118/4/e2016976118

16. Bureau of Labor Statistics (2020, May). *Learn more, earn more: Education leads to higher wages, lower unemployment.* Washington, DC: BLS. https://www.bls.gov/careeroutlook/2020/data-on-display/education-pays.htm (citation is from the chart option).

17. United States Courts (2021). *The U.S. Constitution: Preamble.* Washington, DC: Administrative Office of the U.S. Courts. https://www.uscourts.gov/about-federal-courts/educational-resources/about-educational-outreach/activity-resources/us

18. Mann, H. (1842). *Fifth annual report of the Board of Education.* Boston, MA: Board of Education. https://archives.lib.state.ma.us/bitstream/handle/2452/204724/ocm07166577_1841.pdf?sequence=1&isAllowed=y. Citation on p. 100–101

19. Schoeni, R., House, J., Kaplan, G., & Pollack, H. (Eds.) (2010). *Making Americans healthier: Social and economic policy as health policy.* New York: Russell Sage Foundation.

STRATEGY 1

1. Frost, R. (2021). *The death of the hired hand.* Chicago, IL: The Poetry Foundation. https://www.poetryfoundation.org/poems/44261/the-death-of-the-hired-man

2. Galvin, G. (2018, July 10). A split over safe havens. *U.S. News and World Report.* https://www.usnews.com/news/healthiest-communities/articles/2018-07-10/baby-boxes-safe-haven-laws-a-last-resort-to-curb-infant-abandonment

3. McCall, R. (2011). Research, practice, and policy perspectives on issues of children without permanent parental care. *Monographs of the Society for Research*

in Child Development 76(4), 223–272. https://dx.doi.org/10.1111/j.1540-5834.2011.00634.x

4. I was shocked to learn that baby boxes have been installed in some fire stations so that parents who want to abandon their children have a safe place to do so. See Celeste, E. (2016, May 25). Baby box offers "safe haven" for abandoned newborns. *Voice of America*. https://www.voanews.com/usa/baby-box-offers-safe-haven-abandoned-newborns

5. Skeels, H. (1966). Adult status of children with contrasting early life experiences: A follow-up study. *Monographs of the Society for Research in Child Development 31*(3), 1–65.

6. Skeels, H. (1966). Adult status of children with contrasting early life experiences: A follow-up study. *Monographs of the Society for Research in Child Development 31*(3), 1–65.

7. Skeels, H. (1966). Adult status of children with contrasting early life experiences: A follow-up study. *Monographs of the Society for Research in Child Development 31*(3), 1–65. Data from pp. 21–26.

8. Skeels, H. (1966). Adult status of children with contrasting early life experiences: A follow-up study. *Monographs of the Society for Research in Child Development 31*(3), 1–65. Citations on p. 55.

9. Skeels, H. (1966). Adult status of children with contrasting early life experiences: A follow-up study. *Monographs of the Society for Research in Child Development 31*(3), 1–65. Citations on pp. 54–55.

10. Skeels, H. (1966). Adult status of children with contrasting early life experiences: A follow-up study. *Monographs of the Society for Research in Child Development 31*(3), 1–65.

11. Nisbett, R. (2009). *Intelligence and how to get it*. New York: W.W. Norton.

12. *The Therapeutic Care Journal* (2009, June 1). Adult status of children with contrasting early experience by Harold M. Skeels. Witney, UK: The Mulberry Bush Organization. https://www.thetcj.org/child-care-history-policy/adult-status-of-children-with-contrasting-early-experience-by-harold-m-skeels#google_vignette

13. Mackes, N., Golm, D., Sarkar, S., Kumsta, R., Rutter, M., Fairchild, G., Mehta, M., Sonuga-Barke, E., & ERA Young Adult Follow Up Team (2020, January 6). Early childhood deprivation is associated with alterations in adult brain structure despite subsequent environmental enrichment. *Proceedings of the National Academy of Sciences of the United States of America*. https://www.pnas.org/content/117/1/641

14. Twardosz, S., & Lutzker, J. (2010). Child maltreatment and the developing brain: A review of neuroscience perspectives, *Aggression and Violent Behavior 15* (1), 59–68.

15. Better brains for babies (2021). *Better Brains for Babies Website*. https://www.bbbgeorgia.org

16. Peabody College (2021). *Early childhood environments*. Nashville, TN: Vanderbilt University. https://iris.peabody.vanderbilt.edu/module/env/cresource/q1/p01/

17. Duncan, G., Brooks-Gunn, J., & Kato Klebanov, P. (1994). Economic deprivation and early child development. *Child Development 65*, 296–318.

18. Studies abound about the positive correlations among a strong home environment, health, and well-being. Here's two good ones with radically different perspectives, but similar conclusions: Baharudin, R., & Luster, T. (1998). Factors related to the quality of the home environment and children's achievement. *Journal of Family Issues 19*(4), 375–403; Chang, K., Wong, K., Wong, Y., Ho, H., Wong, M., Ho, Y., Yuen, W., Siu, Y., & Yang, L. (2020). The impact of the environment on quality of life and mediating effects of sleep and stress. *Health Economics & Outcomes Research*. https://research.polyu.edu.hk/en/publications/the-impact-of-the-environment-on-quality-of-life-and-mediating-ef

19. Peabody College (2021). *Early childhood environments*. Nashville, TN: Vanderbilt University. https://iris.peabody.vanderbilt.edu/module/env/cresource/q1/p01/

20. Better brains for babies (2021). *Better Brains for Babies Website*. https://www.bbbgeorgia.org

21. Villarica, H. (2011, August 17). Maslow 2.0: A new and improved recipe for happiness. *The Atlantic*. https://www.theatlantic.com/health/archive/2011/08/maslow-20-a-new-and-improved-recipe-for-happiness/243486/#.TkvKIRv8USE.facebook

22. Maslow, A. (1943). A theory of human motivation. *Psychological Review 50*, 370–396.

23. Bridgman, T., Cummings, S., & Ballard, J. (2018). Who built Maslow's pyramid? *Academy of Management Learning and Education 18*(1), 81–98.

24. Wren, D., & Bedeian, A. (2009). *The evolution of management thought*. New York: Wiley.

25. Maslow, A. (1943). A theory of human motivation. *Psychological Review 50*, 370–396. Citation on p. 388.

26. Tay, L., & Diener, E. (2011). Needs and subjective well-being around the world. *Journal of Personality and Social Psychology 101*(2), 354–365.

27. Feeding America (2018). *Children food insecurity*. https://www.feedingamerica.org/sites/default/files/research/map-the-meal-gap/2016/2016-map-the-meal-gap-child-food-insecurity.pdf

28. Maslow, A. (1954). *Motivation and personality*. New York: Harpers.

29. Wickham, J. (2021). *Is having a sense of belonging important?* Mayo Clinic Health System. https://www.mayoclinichealthsystem.org/hometown-health/speaking-of-health/is-having-a-sense-of-belonging-important

30. Taormina, R., & Gao, J. (2013). Maslow and the motivation hierarchy: Measuring satisfaction of the needs. *American Journal of Psychology 126*(2), 155–177.

STRATEGY 2

1. Caldwell, B. M., & Bradley, R. H. (2016). *Home observation for measurement of the environment: Administration manual*. Tempe, AZ: Family & Human Dynamics Research Institute, Arizona State University. See also: Bureau of Labor Statistics

(2021). *National longitudinal studies: The home*. Washington, DC: BLS. https://www.nlsinfo.org/content/cohorts/nlsy79-children/topical-guide/assessments/home-home-observation-measurement

2. Totsika, V., & Sylva, K. (2004). The home observation for measurement of the environment revisited. *Child and Adolescent Mental Health 9*(1), 25–35. Citation on p. 25.

3. Jordan, M. (1997, May 19). Cited in Zorn, E. Without failure, Jordan would be false idol. *Chicago Tribune*. https://www.chicagotribune.com/news/ct-xpm-1997-05-19-9705190096-story.html

4. Shiffron, H., Liss, M., Miles-McLean, H., Geary, K., Erchull, M., & Tashner, T. (2014). Helping or hovering? The effects of helicopter parenting on college students' well-being. *Journal of Child and Family Studies 23*, 548–557.

5. Bradley, R., & Caldwell, B. (1984). The relation of infants' home environments to achievement test performance in first grade: A follow-up study. *Child Development 55*, 803–809. Citation from p. 803.

6. Otero, G. A., Pliego-Rivero, F. B., Fernández, T., & Ricardo, J. (2003). EEG development in children with sociocultural disadvantages: a follow-up study. *Clinical Neurophysiology: Official Journal of the International Federation of Clinical Neurophysiology 114*(10), 1918–1925. Citation on p. 1918. Citation on p. 1919.

7. Bradley, R. H., Caldwell, B. M., Rock, S. L., Ramey, C. T., Barnard, K. E., Gray, C., Hammond, M., Mitchell, S., Gottfried, A., Siegel, L., & Johnson, D. L. (1989). Home environment and cognitive development in the first 3 years of life: A collaborative study involving six sites and three ethnic groups in North America. *Developmental Psychology 25*(2), 217–235. Citation on p. 221.

8. Ryan, R., O'Farrelly, C., & Ramchandani, P. (2017). Parenting and child mental health. *London Journal of Primary Care 9*(6), 86–94. https://www.ncbi.nlm.nih.gov/pmc/articles/PMC5694794/

9. Hart, B., & Risley, T. (1995). *Meaningful differences in the everyday experience of young American children*. Baltimore, MD: Brookes Publishing.

10. Hart, B., & Risley, T. R. (1995). *Meaningful differences in the everyday experience of young American children*. Baltimore, MD: Brookes Publishing.

11. Hart, B., & Risley, T. (2003, spring). The early catastrophe: The 30 million word gap by age 3. *American Educator*, 4–9. http://www.aft.org//sites/default/files/periodicals/TheEarlyCatastrophe.pdf

12. Of course, 38 points is less than the 54-point differential found by Skeels between adopted and nonadopted children, but 38 points is significant. In fact, it represents more than two standard deviations difference. For more on IQ, see Mensa (2021). *What is IQ?* https://www.mensa.org/iq/what-iq

13. Reardon, S. (2011). *The widening academic achievement gap between the rich and the poor: new evidence and possible explanations*. Palo Alto, CA: Stanford. https://cec1nyc.org/wp-content/uploads/2016/09/sean-reardon-socioeconomic-impact-on-student-achievement.pdf

14. Hart, B., & Risley, T. (2003, spring). The early catastrophe: The 30 million word gap by age 3. *American Educator*, 4–9. http://www.aft.org//sites/default/files/periodicals/TheEarlyCatastrophe.pdf

15. Fox, S. E., Levitt, P., & Nelson, C. A., 3rd (2010). How the timing and quality of early experiences influence the development of brain architecture. *Child Development 81*(1), 28–40. https://www.ncbi.nlm.nih.gov/pmc/articles/PMC2846084/

16. Nelson, C., Zeanah, C., & Fox, N. (2019). How early experience shapes human development: The case of psychosocial deprivation. *Neural Plasticity 2019.* https://pubmed.ncbi.nlm.nih.gov/30774652/

17. Tierney, A., & Nelson, C. (2009). Brain development and the role of experience in the early years. *Zero to Three 30*(2), 9–13.

18. McDaniel, B. (2019, April 26). Parent distraction with phones, reasons for use, and impacts on parenting and child outcomes: A review of the emerging research. *Human Behavior and Emerging Technologies.* https://onlinelibrary.wiley.com/doi/10.1002/hbe2.139

19. Morris, E. (1979). *The rise of Theodore Roosevelt.* New York: Modern Library.

20. Morris, E. (2001). *Theodore Rex.* New York: Random House.

21. Johnston, H. (1919, January 16). Theodore Roosevelt. *Nature 102*, 389–390. https://www.nature.com/articles/102389a0

STRATEGY 3

1. Nagy, W., Anderson, R., & Herman, P. (1987). Learning word meanings from context during normal reading. *American Educational Research Journal 24*, 237–270.

2. Hruby, G., & Goswami, U. (2011). Neruoscience and reading: A review for reading education researchers. *Reading Research Quarterly 46*(2), 156–172.

3. Baines, L. (1993). *Aspects of language in literature and film.* (Doctoral dissertation. The University of Texas at Austin). Dissertation Abstracts International *54*(4), 1268.

4. Cunningham, A., & Stanovich, K. (1998, Spring/Summer). What reading does for the mind. *American Educator,* 1–8.

5. Anderson, R., & Freebody, P. (1981). Vocabulary knowledge. In J. Guthrie (Ed.), *Comprehension and teaching: Research reviews* (pp. 77–117). Newark, DE: International Reading Association.

6. Baines, L. (1998). The future of the written word. In J. Simmons & L. Baines (Eds.), *Language study in middle school, high school, and beyond,* pp. 190–214. Newark, DE: National Reading Association.

7. Baines, L. (1993). *Aspects of language in literature and film.* Dissertation. Austin, TX: University of Texas at Austin.

8. Schleicher, A. (2018). *World class: How to build a 21st-century school system, strong performers and successful reformers in education.* Paris, France: OECD Publishing. https://dx.doi.org/10.1787/9789264300002-en

9. National Center for Education Statistics (2021). *PISA 2018 U.S.A. results.* Washington, DC: NCES. https://nces.ed.gov/surveys/pisa/pisa2018/#/

10. OECD (2019). PISA 2018 assessment and analytical framework. Paris, France: OECD Publishing; data on this chart is taken from Evans, M., Kelley, J., &

Sikora, J. (2014). Scholarly culture and academic performance in 42 nations. *Social Forces.* https://academic.oup.com/sf/article/92/4/1573/2235883

11. Baines, L. A. (2007). Achieving more by doing less. *Phi Delta Kappan 89*(2), 98–101.

12. Baines, L. A. (2008). Achieving more by doing less. *Education Digest 73*, 23–26. Citation on p. 25.

13. Dahl, R. (1996). *The great automatic grammatizator.* New York: Viking.

14. Johns Hopkins Medicine (2021). How the brain works. https://www.hopkinsmedicine.org/neurology_neurosurgery/centers_clinics/brain_tumor/about-brain-tumors/how-the-brain-works.html

15. Barquero L., Davis N., & Cutting L. (2014). Neuroimaging of reading intervention: A systematic review and activation likelihood estimate meta-analysis. *PLOS ONE 9*(1), e83668. https://doi.org/10.1371/journal.pone.0083668. Citation from the abstract.

16. Menary, K., Collins, P. F., Porter, J. N., Muetzel, R., Olson, E. A., Kumar, V., Steinbach, M., Lim, K. O., & Luciana, M. (2013). Associations between cortical thickness and general intelligence in children, adolescents and young adults. *Intelligence, 41*(5), 597–606. https://doi.org/10.1016/j.intell.2013.07.010

17. Edelman, G. (1987). *Neural Darwinism.* New York: Basic Books.

18. Otero, G. A., Pliego-Rivero, F. B., Fernández, T., & Ricardo, J. (2003). EEG development in children with sociocultural disadvantages: A follow-up study. *Clinical Neurophysiology: Official Journal of the International Federation of Clinical Neurophysiology 114*(10), 1918–1925. Citation on p. 1918, 1919, 1923.

19. Bradley, R., Caldwell, B., & Rock, S. (1988). Home environment and school performance: A ten-year follow-up and examination of three models of environmental action. *Child Development 59*, 852–867.

20. Otero, G. A., Pliego-Rivero, F. B., Fernández, T., & Ricardo, J. (2003). EEG development in children with sociocultural disadvantages: A follow-up study. *Clinical Neurophysiology: Official Journal of the International Federation of Clinical Neurophysiology 114*(10), 1918–1925. Citation on p. 1918.

21. Bradley, R. H., Caldwell, B. M., Rock, S. L., Ramey, C. T., Barnard, K. E., Gray, C., Hammond, M., Mitchell, S., Gottfried, A., Siegel, L., & Johnson, D. L. (1989). Home environment and cognitive development in the first 3 years of life: A collaborative study involving six sites and three ethnic groups in North America. *Developmental Psychology 25*(2), 217–235. Citation on p. 232.

22. Bradley, R. H., Caldwell, B. M., Rock, S. L., Ramey, C. T., Barnard, K. E., Gray, C., Hammond, M., Mitchell, S., Gottfried, A., Siegel, L., & Johnson, D. L. (1989). Home environment and cognitive development in the first 3 years of life: A collaborative study involving six sites and three ethnic groups in North America. *Developmental Psychology 25*(2), 217–235. Citation on p. 233.

23. Hair, E., & Graziano, W. (2003). Self-esteem, personality and achievement in high school: A prospective longitudinal study in Texas. *Journal of Personality 71*(5), 971–994; see also Russ, S. (2004). *Play in child development and psychotherapy: Toward empirically supported practice.* Mahwah, NJ: Lawrence.

24. Oppenheim, J. (1984). *Kids and play.* New York: Ballantine.

STRATEGY 4

1. American Psychological Association (2019, May). Media use in childhood: evidence-based recommendations for caregivers. https://www.apa.org/pi/families/resources/newsletter/2019/05/media-use-childhood

2. Rideout, V., & Robb, M. B. (2020). *The common sense census: Media use by kids age zero to eight, 2020.* San Francisco, CA: Common Sense Media. Data from page 19. https://www.commonsensemedia.org/sites/default/files/uploads/research/2020_zero_to_eight_census_final_web.pdf

3. Baines, L. A. (2013). Then, let them eat screens. *Teachers College Record.* http://www.tcrecord.org ID NUMBER: 17112.

4. Reportlinker (2017, January 26). Smartphone statistics: For most users, it's a "round-the-clock" connection. *Reportlinker Insight.* https://www.reportlinker.com/insight/smartphone-connection.html

5. Rideout, V., & Robb, M. B. (2020). *The common sense census: Media use by kids age zero to eight, 2020.* San Francisco, CA: Common Sense Media. Citation on page i. https://www.commonsensemedia.org/sites/default/files/uploads/research/2020_zero_to_eight_census_final_web.pdf

6. Rideout, V., & Robb, M. B. (2020). *The common sense census: Media use by kids age zero to eight, 2020.* San Francisco, CA: Common Sense Media. Citation on page 3. https://www.commonsensemedia.org/sites/default/files/uploads/research/2020_zero_to_eight_census_final_web.pdf

7. American Psychological Association (2019, May). Media use in childhood: Evidence-based recommendations for caregivers. https://www.apa.org/pi/families/resources/newsletter/2019/05/media-use-childhood

8. Hutton, J., Dudley, J., Horowitz-Kraus, T., DeWitt, T., & Holland, S. (2020). Associations between screen-based media use and brain white matter integrity in preschool-aged children. *JAMA Pediatrics 174*(1). https://jamanetwork.com/journals/jamapediatrics/fullarticle/2754101

9. Robinson, T. N., Banda, J. A., Hale, L., Lu, A. S., Fleming-Milici, F., Calvert, S. L., & Wartella, E. (2017). Screen media exposure and obesity in children and adolescents. *Pediatrics, 140*(Suppl 2), S97–S101. https://www.ncbi.nlm.nih.gov/pmc/articles/PMC5769928/

10. Tamana S., Ezeugwu V., Chikuma J., Lefebvre D., Azad M., Moraes, T., Subbarao, P., Becker, A., Turvey, S., Sears, M., Dick, B., Carson, V., Rasmussen, C., Pei, J., & Mandhane, P. (2019) Screen-time is associated with inattention problems in preschoolers: Results from the CHILD birth cohort study. *PLOS ONE 14*(4). https://journals.plos.org/plosone/article?id=10.1371/journal.pone.0213995

11. Hisler, G., Hasler, B., Franzen, P., Clark, D., & Twenge, J. (2020, December). Screen media use and sleep disturbance symptom severity in children. *Sleep Health 6*(6), 731–742; Bruni, O., Sette, S., Fontanesi, L., Baiocco, R., Laghi, F., & Baumgartner, E. (2015). Technology use and sleep quality in preadolescence and adolescence. *Journal of Clinical Sleep Medicine: JCSM: Official Publication of the American Academy of Sleep Medicine 11*(12), 1433–1441.

12. Auxier, B., Anderson, M., Perrin, A., & Turner, E. (2020, July 28). *Parenting children in the age of screens.* Washington, DC: Pew Research Center.

https://www.pewresearch.org/internet/2020/07/28/parenting-children-in-the-age-of-screens/

13. Auxier, B., Anderson, M., Perrin, A., & Turner, E. (2020, July 28). *Parenting children in the age of screens*. Washington, DC: Pew Research Center. https://www.pewresearch.org/internet/2020/07/28/parenting-children-in-the-age-of-screens/. Citation on page 5.

14. Auxier, B., Anderson, M., Perrin, A., & Turner, E. (2020, July 28). *Parenting children in the age of screens*. Washington, DC: Pew Research Center. https://www.pewresearch.org/internet/2020/07/28/parenting-children-in-the-age-of-screens/. Citation on page 4.

15. American Academy of Child and Adolescent Psychiatry (2020, February). *Screen time and children*. https://www.aacap.org/AACAP/Families_and_Youth/Facts_for_Families/FFF-Guide/Children-And-Watching-TV-054.aspx

16. Milliot, J. (2020, July 10). Print units post surprising increase in first half of 2020. *Publisher's Weekly*. https://www.publishersweekly.com/pw/by-topic/industry-news/bookselling/article/83829-print-units-post-surprising-increase-in-first-half-of-2020.html

17. Rideout, V., & Robb, M. B. (2019). *The common sense census: Media use by tweens and teens, 2019*. San Francisco, CA: Common Sense Media.

18. Bureau of Labor Statistics (2020). *Table 11A: Time spent in leisure and sports activities for the civilian population by selected characteristics, averages per day, 2019*. Washington, DC: BLS. https://www.bls.gov/news.release/atus.t11a.htm

19. Bureau of Labor Statistics (2021). *American time use survey lexicon*. Washington, DC: U.S. Government Printing. The definition for reading is found on p. 51.

20. Sparks, S. (2019, November 8). Screen time up as reading scores drop. Is there a link? *Education Week*. https://www.edweek.org/teaching-learning/screen-time-up-as-reading-scores-drop-is-there-a-link/2019/11

21. Lanier, J. (2017, December 16). In Bernard, Z., & Tweedie, S. The father of virtual reality sounds off on the changing culture of Silicon Valley. *Business Insider*. https://www.businessinsider.com/jaron-lanier-interview-on-silicon-valley-culture-metoo-backlash-ai-and-the-future-2017-12

22. Baron, Z. (2020, August 24). The conscience of Silicon Valley. *GQ*. https://www.gq.com/story/jaron-lanier-tech-oracle-profile

23. Akhtar, A., & Ward, M. (2020, May 15). Bill Gates and Steve Jobs raised their kids with limited tech—and it should have been a red flag about our own smartphone use. *Business Insider*. https://www.businessinsider.com/screen-time-limits-bill-gates-steve-jobs-red-flag-2017-10; see also Clement, J., & Miles, M. (2017). *Screen schooled*. Chicago, IL: Chicago Review Press.

STRATEGY 5

1. Schack, T., & Mechsner, F. (2006). Representation of motor skills in human long-term memory. *Neuroscience Letters 391*(3), 77–81.

2. Piaget, J. (1963). *The origins of intelligence in children.* New York: W. W. Norton & Company, Inc.

3. Harvard University Center on the Developing Child (2020). *InBrief: The impact of early adversity on children's development.* Cambridge, MA: Harvard University. https://developingchild.harvard.edu/resources/inbrief-the-impact-of-early-adversity-on-childrens-development/

4. National Center for Learning Disabilities (2014). *The state of learning disabilities: Facts, trends and emerging issues* (3rd ed.). New York: National Center for Learning Disabilities. http://www.ncld.org/wp-content/uploads/2014/11/2014-State-of-LD.pdf

5. Baines, L. A., & Slutsky, R. (2009, Winter). Developing the sixth sense: Play. *Educational Horizons,* 97–101.

6. Jamison, K. (2004). *Exuberance.* New York: Alfred Knopf.

7. Murray, R., & Ramstetter, C. (2013, January). The crucial role of recess in school. *Pediatrics 131*(1), 183–188.

8. Johnson, I., & Ginicola, M. (2019, January). Gym class is dead—but long live physical education. *Principal Leadership 19.* https://www.nassp.org/publication/principal-leadership/volume-19-2018-2019/principal-leadership-january-2019/fit-to-learn-january-2019/

9. Pontifex, M., Hillman, C., Fernhall, Bo, & Thompson, K. (2009). The effect of acute aerobic and resistance exercise on working memory. *Medicine and Science in Sports and Exercise 41*(4), 927–934.

10. Brown, S. (2010). *Play.* New York: Avery Publishing.

11. Yang, L., Chao, C., Kantor, E., Nguyen, L., Zheng, X., Park, Y., Giovannucci, E., Matthews, C., Colditz, G., & Cao, Y. (2019). Trends in sedentary behavior among the US population, 2001-2016. *JAMA 321*(16), 1587–1597.

12. Yang, L., Chao, C., Kantor, E., Nguyen, L., Zheng, X., Park, Y., Giovannucci, E., Matthews, C., Colditz, G., & Cao, Y. (2019). Trends in sedentary behavior among the US population, 2001-2016. *JAMA 321*(16), 1587–1597. Citation is on p. 1588.

13. United States Environmental Protection Agency (1989). *Report to Congress on indoor air quality: Volume 2.* Washington, DC: EPA.

14. De La Cruz, D. (2017, March 21). Why kids shouldn't sit still in class. *New York Times.* https://www.nytimes.com/2017/03/21/well/family/why-kids-shouldnt-sit-still-in-class.html

15. Washington State Parks (2021). *No child left inside program.* Seattle, WA. https://parks.state.wa.us/972/No-Child-Left-Inside

16. Louv, R. (2008). *Last child in the woods: Saving our children from nature-deficit-disorder.* New York: Workman Publishing.

17. Berman, M. G., Jonides, J., & Kaplan, S. (2008). The cognitive benefits of interacting with nature. *Psychological Science 19,* 1207–1212.

18. Schutte, A. R., Torquati, J. C., & Beattie, H. L. (2017). Impact of urban nature on executive functioning in early and middle childhood. *Environment and Behavior 49*(1), 3–30. https://journals.sagepub.com/doi/full/10.1177/0013916515603095

19. Schutte, A. R., Torquati, J. C., & Beattie, H. L. (2017). Impact of urban nature on executive functioning in early and middle childhood. *Environment and Behavior 49*(1), 3–30. https://journals.sagepub.com/doi/full/10.1177/0013916515603095

20. Berto, R. (2005). Exposure to restorative environments helps restore attentional capacity. *Journal of Environmental Psychology 25*, 249–259.

21. Clark, E., & Dumas, A. (2020). Children's active outdoor play: "good" mothering and the organization of children's free time. *Sociology of Health & Illness 42*(6), 1229–1242. Citation on p. 1229. https://onlinelibrary.wiley.com/doi/full/10.1111/1467-9566.13107, p. 1230.

22. McAnally, H. M., Robertson, L. A. & Hancox, R. J. (2018). Effects of an outdoor education programme on creative thinking and well-being in adolescent boys. *New Zealand Journal of Educational Studies 53*, 241–255. Citation on p. 241.

23. Fuegen, K., & Breitenbecher, K. (2018). Walking and being outdoors in nature increase positive affect and energy. *Ecopsychology 10*, 14–25.

24. Atchley, R.; Strayer D.; & Atchley, P. (2012). Creativity in the wild: Improving creative reasoning through immersion in natural settings. *PLoS ONE 7*(12). https://journals.plos.org/plosone/article?id=10.1371/journal.pone.0051474

25. Clark, E., & Dumas, A. (2020). Children's active outdoor play: "good" mothering and the organization of children's free time. *Sociology of Health & Illness 42*(6), 1229–1242. Citation on p. 1229. https://onlinelibrary.wiley.com/doi/full/10.1111/1467-9566.13107, p. 1230.

26. McCormick, R. (2017). Does access to green space impact the mental well-being of children: A systematic review. *Journal of Pediatric Nursing 37*, 3–7. https://www.sciencedirect.com/science/article/pii/S0882596317301859). Citation on p. 3. See also: McAnally, H. M., Robertson, L. A. & Hancox, R. J. (2018). Effects of an outdoor education programme on creative thinking and well-being in adolescent boys. *New Zealand Journal of Educational Studies 53*, 241–255. Citation on p. 254.

27. Fuegen, K., & Breitenbecher, K. (2018). Walking and being outdoors in nature increase positive affect and energy. *Ecopsychology 10*, 14–25. See discussion on p. 251.

28. Mackey, N. (2021, April 12). Cited in Hsu, H., "The long song." *New Yorker*, p. 29.

29. Richardson, R. (1995). *Emerson: The mind on fire*. Berkeley: University of California Press.

30. Emerson, R. (1836, accessed 2021). *Essay on nature*. https://archive.vcu.edu/english/engweb/transcendentalism/authors/emerson/essays/naturetext.html

31. The House of Ralph Waldo Emerson (2021). *Happy is the house that shelters a friend*. Concord, MA: Ralph Waldo Emerson Memorial Foundation.

32. Emerson, R. (2000). *The essential writings of Ralph Waldo Emerson*. New York: Modern Library.

STRATEGY 6

1. Schlam, C. (2020). *The joy of art*. New York: Simon & Schuster.

2. Cornell Law School (2021). Definitions: *20 U.S. Code 952*. https://www.law.cornell.edu/uscode/text/20/952

3. Noddings, N. (2012). The caring relation in teaching, *Oxford Review of Education 38*(6), 771–781.

4. Jason, Z. (2017, Winter). Bored out of their minds. *Ed.: Harvard Ed Magazine*. Cambridge, MA: Harvard University. https://www.gse.harvard.edu/news/ed/17/01/bored-out-their-minds

5. Gernhardt, A., Rübeling, H., & Keller, H. (2015). Cultural perspectives on children's tadpole drawings: at the interface between representation and production. *Frontiers in Psychology 6*(812). https://doi.org/10.3389/fpsyg.2015.00812

6. Colbert, C., & Taunton, M. (1992). *Developmentally appropriate practices for the visual arts education of young children*. Reston, VA: National Arts Education Association.

7. Cain, A. (2017, August 25). What do the childhood works of famous artists look like? *Artsy*. https://www.artsy.net/article/artsy-editorial-childhood-works-famous-artists-like

8. Cabanne, P. (1977). *Pablo Picasso: His life and times*. New York: Morrow

9. Voorhies, J. (2004, October). *Pablo Picasso (1881–1973)*. New York: Metropolitan Museum of Art. https://www.metmuseum.org/toah/hd/pica/hd_pica.htm

10. Waller, D. (2013). *Becoming a profession: the history of art therapy in Britain 1940–82*. London: Routledge.

11. Regev, D., & Cohen-Yatziv, L. (2018). Effectiveness of art therapy with adult clients in 2018-What progress has been made? *Frontiers in Psychology 9*(1531). https://doi.org/10.3389/fpsyg.2018.01531

12. Ketch, R., Rubin, R., Baker, M., Sones, A., & Ames, D. (2015). Art appreciation for veterans with severe mental illness in a VA psychosocial rehabilitee and recovery center. *Arts & Health: International Journal for Research, Policy & Practice 7*(2), 172–181.

13. Staricoff, R. & Clift, S. (2011). *Arts and music in healthcare: An overview of the medical literature: 2004–2011*. London: Chelsea and Westminster Health Charity. Citation on pp. 4–5. http://www.lahf.org.uk/sites/default/files/Chelsea%20and%20Westminster%20Literature%20Review%20Staricoff%20and%20Clift%20FINAL.pdf

14. Stuckey, H. L., & Nobel, J. (2010). The connection between art, healing, and public health: A review of current literature. *American Journal of Public Health 100*(2), 254–263. https://doi.org/10.2105/AJPH.2008.156497

15. Jensen, A., & Bonde, L. O. (2018). The use of arts interventions for mental health and wellbeing in health settings. *Perspectives in Public Health 138*(4), 209–214. https://doi.org/10.1177/1757913918772602

16. Kaimal, G., Ray, K., & Muniz, J. (2016) Reduction of cortisol levels and participants' responses following art making, *Art Therapy 33*(2), 74–80. Citation on page 74.

17. Stuckey, H. L., & Nobel, J. (2010). The connection between art, healing, and public health: a review of current literature. *American Journal of Public Health 100*(2), 254–263. https://doi.org/10.2105/AJPH.2008.156497

18. Lee, J., Choi, M. Y., Kim, Y. B., Sun, J., Park, E. J., Kim, J. H., Kang, M., & Koom, W. S. (2017). Art therapy based on appreciation of famous paintings and its effect on distress among cancer patients. *Quality of Life Research: An International Journal of Quality of Life Aspects of Treatment, Care and Rehabilitation 26*(3), 707–715. https://doi.org/10.1007/s11136-016-1473-5

19. Qiu, H.-Z., Ye, Z.-J., Liang, M.-Z., Huang, Y.-Q., Liu, W., & Lu, Z.-D. (2017). Effect of an art brut therapy program called go beyond the schizophrenia (GBTS) on prison inmates with schizophrenia in mainland China—A randomized, longitudinal, and controlled trial. *Clinical Psychology & Psychotherapy 24*(95), 1069–1078. https://doi.org/10.1002/cpp.2069

20. Staricoff R. & Clift, S. (2011). *Arts and music in healthcare: An overview of the medical literature: 2004–2011*. London: Chelsea and Westminster Health Charity.

21. Stuckey, H. L., & Nobel, J. (2010). The connection between art, healing, and public health: A review of current literature. *American Journal of Public Health, 100*(2), 254–263. https://doi.org/10.2105/AJPH.2008.156497

22. Richardson, C. (2015). *Expressive arts therapy for traumatized children and adolescents*. London: Routledge.

23. Merton, T. (2005). *No man is an island*. Boulder, CO: Shambhala. Citation is on page 35.

24. Dowell, S. (2018, December 4). Beaten, starved and tortured: The horrifying story of Hitler's concentration camp for children. *The First News*. https://www.thefirstnews.com/article/the-horrifying-story-of-hitlers-concentration-camp-for-children-3622

25. Sharon, A., Levav, I., Brodsky, J., Shemesh, A., & Kohn, R. (2009). Psychiatric disorders and other health dimensions among Holocaust survivors 6 decades later. *British Journal of Psychiatry 195*(4), 331–335.

26. Naumburg, M. (1943). Children's art expression and war. *Nervous Child 2*(1), 360–373.

27. Naumburg, M. (2001). Spontaneous art in education and psychotherapy. *American Journal of Art Therapy 40*, 46–64.

28. Naumburg, M. (1943). Children's art expression and war. *Nervous Child 2*(1), 360–373.

29. Malchiodi, C. (2003). Preface. In C. Malchiodi (Ed.), *Handbook of art therapy*, p. ix. New York: Guilford Press.

STRATEGY 7

1. Sweeney-Brown, C. (2005). Music and medicine. In M. Pavlicivic (Ed.), *Music therapy in children's hospices* (pp. 48–61). London: Jessica Kingsley Publishers.

2. Sweeney-Brown, C. (2005). Music and medicine. In M. Pavlicivic (Ed.), *Music therapy in children's hospices* (pp. 48–61). London: Jessica Kingsley Publishers. Citation on p. 57.

3. Hudgens, C. (1987, May). *A study of the Kodaly approach to music teaching and an investigation of four approaches to the teaching of selected skills in first grade music classes*. Dissertation. Denton, TX: University of North Texas.

4. Sala, G., & Gobet, F. (2017). When the music's over. Does music skill transfer to children's and young adolescents' cognitive and academic skills? A meta-analysis. *Educational Research Review 20*, 55–67. doi: 10.1016/j.edurev.2016.11.005

5. Matthews, J. (2019, July 18). America's indefensible defense budget. *New York Review of Books*. https://www.nybooks.com/articles/2019/07/18/americas-indefensible-defense-budget/

6. General Accounting Office (2017). *Military bands*. Washington, DC: GAO. GAO-17-657.

7. Biggs, M., Homan, S., Dedrick, R., Minick, V., & Rasinski, T. (2008). Using an interactive singing software program: A comparative study of struggling middle school readers. *Reading Psychology 29*, 195–213.

8. Biggs, M., Homan, S., Dedrick, R., Minick, V., & Rasinski, T. (2008). Using an interactive singing software program: A comparative study of struggling middle school readers. *Reading Psychology 29*, 195–213.

9. Staricoff, R. L. (2004). *Arts in health: A review of the medical literature. Research report 36*. London: Arts Council England. http://www.artscouncil.org.uk/ publication_archive/arts-in-health-a-review-of-the-medical-literature/. Also: Staricoff, R. L. (2006). Arts in health: the value of evaluation. *Journal of the Royal Society for the Promotion of Health*, *126*(3), 116–120. https://doi.org/10.1177/1466424006064300

10. Wu, K., Anderson, J., Townsend, J., Frazier, T., Brandt, A. & Karmonik, C. (2019). Characterization of functional brain connectivity towards optimization of music selection for therapy: a fMRI study. *International Journal of Neuroscience 129*(9), 882–889. Citation on p. 882.

11. Kraus, N. Slater, J., Thompson, E., Hornickel, J., Strait, D., Nicol, T., & White-Schwoch, T. (2014, September). *Journal of Neuroscience 34*(36), 11913–11918. https://doi.org/10.1523/JNEUROSCI.1881-14.2014

12. Staricoff, R. & Clift, S. (2011). *Arts and music in healthcare: An overview of the medical literature: 2004-2011*. London: Chelsea and Westminster Health Charity. Citation on page 8. http://www.lahf.org.uk/sites/default/files/Chelsea%20and %20Westminster%20Literature%20Review%20Staricoff%20and%20Clift %20FINAL.pdf

13. Staricoff, R. & Clift, S. (2011). *Arts and music in healthcare: An overview of the medical literature: 2004-2011*. London: Chelsea and Westminster Health Charity. Citation on page 255. http://www.lahf.org.uk/sites/default/files/Chelsea%20and %20Westminster%20Literature%20Review%20Staricoff%20and%20Clift %20FINAL.pdf

14. Staricoff, R. & Clift, S. (2011). *Arts and music in healthcare: An overview of the medical literature: 2004-2011*. London: Chelsea and Westminster Health Charity. Citation on page 82. http://www.lahf.org.uk/sites/default/files/Chelsea%20and %20Westminster%20Literature%20Review%20Staricoff%20and%20Clift %20FINAL.pdf

15. Winner, E., & Martino, G. (2000). Giftedness in non-academic domains: The case of the visual arts and music. In K. Heller, F. Monks, R. Sternberg, & R. Subotnik (Eds.), *International handbook of giftedness and talent*. New York: Elsevier, pp. 95–110. Citation on p. 106.

16. Winner, E., & Martino, G. (2000). Giftedness in non-academic domains: The case of the visual arts and music. In K. Heller, F. Monks, R. Sternberg, & R. Subotnik (Eds.), *International handbook of giftedness and talent*. New York: Elsevier, pp. 95–110. Citation on p. 107.

17. Plato (2016). *The Republic*, B. Jowett (Translator). https://www.gutenberg.org/files/1497/1497-h/1497-h.htm#link2H_4_0006. The passage comes from Book 3.

18. Caeyers, J. (2020). *Beethoven: A life*. Berkeley, CA: University of California Press.

19. Langer, S. (1942). *Philosophy in a new key*. Cambridge, MA: Harvard University Press. Citation on page 243.

20. Fletcher, T. (1998). *Dear boy: The life of Keith Moon*. Chicago: Independent Publishers Group.

STRATEGY 8

1. *Oxford English Dictionary* (2021). Entry for *homophily*. https://www.oed.com/view/Entry/68972848?rskey=5AocTz&result=2#eid

2. Byrne, C. (2018, September 5). This basic fact about social networks disadvantages minorities. *Fast Company*. https://www.fastcompany.com/90220470/this-basic-fact-about-social-networks-disadvantages-minorities

3. Laakasuo, M., Rotkirch, A., van Duijn, M., Berg, V., Jokela, M., David-Barrett, T., Miettinen, A., Pearce, E., & Dunbar, R. (2020). Homophily in personality enhances group success among real-life friends. *Frontiers in Psychology 11*, 710. https://doi.org/10.3389/fpsyg.2020.00710

4. Rogers, E. (1965). What are innovators like? In R. Carlson, A. Gallaher, M. Miles, R. Pellegrin, & E. Rogers (Eds.), *Change process in the public schools*. Eugene, OR: Center for the Advanced Study of Educational Administration.

5. Currarini, S., & Mengel, F. (2016). Identity, homophily and in-group bias, *European Economic Review 90*, 40–55. https://doi.org/10.1016/j.euroecorev.2016.02.015

6. Mollica, K., Gray, B., & Treviño, L. (2003). Racial homophily and its persistence in newcomers' social networks. *Organization Science 14*(2), 123–136.

7. Clinton, J., & Roush, C. (2016, August 10). *Poll: persistent partisan divide over 'birther' question, seventy-two percent of registered Republican voters still doubt President Obama's citizenship, according to a recent NBC news|surveymonkey poll*. https://www.nbcnews.com/politics/2016-election/poll-persistent-partisan-divide-over-birther-question-n627446

8. Godwin, R. (2019, July 10). One giant ... lie? Why so many people still think the moon landings were faked. *The Guardian*. https://www.theguardian.com/science/2019/jul/10/one-giant-lie-why-so-many-people-still-think-the-moon-landings-were-faked

9. American Psychological Association Dictionary of Psychology (2021). *Definition of heterophily*. https://dictionary.apa.org/heterophily

10. Edwards-Schachter, M. (2018). The nature and variety of innovation. *International Journal of Innovation Studies 2*(2), 65–79; Rogers, E. (1965). What are innovators like? In R. Carlson, A. Gallaher, M. Miles, R. Pellegrin, & E. Rogers (Eds.), *Change process in the public schools*. Eugene, OR: Center for the Advanced Study of Educational Administration. Citation on p. 58.

11. McKinsey & Company (2020, May). *Diversity wins*. London: McKinsey & Company. https://www.mckinsey.com/~/media/mckinsey/featured%20insights/diversity%20and%20inclusion/diversity%20wins%20how%20inclusion%20matters/diversity-wins-how-inclusion-matters-vf.pdf

12. World Economic Forum (2020). *The future of jobs report*. Cologny, Switzerland: WEF. See chapter 2 for details on needed skills and declining/emerging jobs.

13. Palmer, D., & Menard-Warwick, J. (2012). Short-term study abroad for Texas preservice teachers: On the road from empathy to critical awareness. *Multicultural Education 19*(3), 17–26.

14. McKinsey Global Institute (2018). *Skill shift: Automation and the future of the workplace*. Hong Kong: MGI.

15. Nahon, K., & Hemsley, J. (2014). Homophily in the guise of cross-linking: Political blogs and content. *American Behavioral Scientist 58*(10), 1294–1313.

16. Gundelach, B. (2013). In diversity we trust: The positive effect of ethnic diversity on outgroup trust. *Political Behavior 36*, 125–142. Citation on p. 136.

17. Vozza, S. (2016, January 13). Eight career skills you need to be competitive in 2016, *Fast Company*. https://www.fastcompany.com/3055352/eight-career-skills-you-need-to-be-competitive-in-2016

18. Hansen, J. (2010). Counseling and psychoanalysis: Advancing the value of diversity. *Multicultural Counseling and Development 38*, 16–26.

19. Harari, Y. (2018, August 12). Yuval Noah Harari on what the year 2050 has in store for humankind. *Wired*. https://www.wired.co.uk/article/yuval-noah-harari-extract-21-lessons-for-the-21st-century. The 4Cs showed up years ago in the platform of a reform movement known as the *Partnership for 21st Century Learning*. Although the rights to the Partnership's old material was purchased by a corporation, they could not copyright the 4Cs or the 4Cs' viability for the future. See Schaffhauser, D. (2015, September 2). P21 research series offers advice on 21st century "4Cs." *The Journal*. https://thejournal.com/articles/2015/09/02/p21-research-series-offers-advice-on-21st-century-4cs.aspx

20. American Psychological Association (2021). *Tantrum in the grocery store*. Washington, DC: ACT: A parenting program from APA. https://www.apa.org/act/resources/fact-sheets/challenging-36-months

21. Astington, J. W., & Hughes, C. (2013). Theory of mind: Self-reflection and social understanding. In P. D. Zelazo (Ed.), *Oxford library of psychology. The Oxford handbook of developmental psychology, Vol. 2. Self and other* (pp. 398–424). Oxford, UK: Oxford University Press.

22. Kang, S. (2014, July 3). How travel opens the eyes, minds, and hearts of youngsters. *Psychology Today*. https://www.psychologytoday.com/intl/blog/the-dolphin-way/201407/how-travel-opens-the-eyes-minds-and-hearts-youngsters

23. Pols, J., & Kroon, H. (2007). The importance of holiday trips for people with chronic mental health problems. *Psychiatric Services 58*(2), 262–265.

24. Mezirow, J. (September 1, 1981). A critical theory of adult learning and education. *Adult Education Quarterly 32*(1), 3–24.

25. Kolb, A., & Kolb, D. (2005). Learning styles and learning spaces: Enhancing experiential learning in higher education. *Academy of Management Learning & Education 4*(2), 193–212. Citation on p. 194. http://www.jstor.org/stable/40214287

26. Csikszentmihalyi, M. (1994). *The evolving self.* New York: Harper Perennial.

27. Chen, C., & Petrick, J. (2013). Health and wellness benefits of travel experiences: A literature review. *Journal of Travel Research 52*(6), 709–719.

28. Esalen Institute (2021). *In Memorium: Joseph Campbell (1904 -1987).* San Francisco, CA: Esalen Institute. https://www.esalen.org/memorial/joseph-campbell

29. Chiocca, E. (2018). *Not upgraded tourism: A case study of the effects of a short-term study abroad experience in Israel.* Norman, OK: The University of Oklahoma. Dissertation.

30. Twain, M. (2006, c1884). *Innocents abroad.* The Gutenberg Project. http://www.gutenberg.org/files/3176/3176-h/3176-h.htm

31. Gundelach, B. (2013). In diversity we trust: The positive effect of ethnic diversity on outgroup trust. *Political Behavior 36*, 125–142. Citation on p. 127.

STRATEGY 9

1. Oxford English Dictionary. *Entry for resilience.* https://www.oed.com/view/Entry/163619?redirectedFrom=resilience#eid

2. American Psychological Association (2012). Resilience guide for parents and teachers. Washington, DC: APA. https://www.apa.org/topics/resilience/guide-parents-teachers

3. Henry, M., Shorter, S., Charkoudian, L., Heemstra, J., & Corwin, L. (2019). FAIL is not a four-letter word: A theoretical framework for exploring undergraduate students' approaches to academic challenge and responses to failure in STEM learning environments. *CBE—Life Sciences Education 18*(1), 1–17. Citation on p. 1.

4. Heider, F. (1958). *The psychology of interpersonal relations.* New York: Wiley; Weiner, B. (1992). *Human motivation: Metaphors, theories and research.* Newbury Park, CA: Sage Publications).

5. Henry, M., Shorter, S., Charkoudian, L., Heemstra, J., & Corwin, L. (2019). FAIL is not a four-letter word: A theoretical framework for exploring undergraduate students' approaches to academic challenge and responses to failure in STEM learning environments. *CBE—Life Sciences Education 18*(1), 1–17. Citation on p. 3.

6. Farrington, C., Roderick, M., Allensworth, E., Nagaoka, J., Keyes, T., Johnson, D., & Beechum, N. (2012, June). *Teaching adolescents to become learners: The role of noncognitive factors in shaping school performance: A critical literature review.* Chicago: University of Chicago. https://consortium.uchicago.edu/publications/teaching-adolescents-become-learners-role-noncognitive-factors-shaping-school. Citation on p. 8.

7. Tough, P. (2016). *Helping children succeed.* Boston, MA: Houghton Mifflin Harcourt.

8. Duckworth, A. (2021). Preface to the book *Grit.* New York: Scribner. https://angeladuckworth.com/grit-book-excerpt/

9. Duckworth, A., Peterson, C., Matthews, M., & Kelly, D. (2007). Grit: Perseverance and passion for long-term goals. *Journal of Personality and Social Psychology 92*, 1087–1101.

10. Mischel, W. (2017). *The marshmallow test: Mastering self-control.* New York: Little, Brown and Company. See also: Konnikova, M. (2014, October 14). The

struggles of a psychologist studying self-control. *New Yorker.* https://www.newyorker.com/science/maria-konnikova/struggles-psychologist-studying-self-control

11. Mischel, W., Shoda, Y., & Rodriguez, M. (1989, May). Delay of gratification in children. *Science 244*, 933–938.

12. Baines, L., & McBrayer, D. (2003a). *How to get a life: Empowering wisdom for the heart and soul.* Atlanta, GA: Humanics; Baines, L., & McBrayer, D. (2003b). *How to get a life: Empowering wisdom from thinkers and writers.* Atlanta, GA: Humanics.

13. Buscaglia, L. (2003). Cited in Short, S., Leo F. Buscaglia. In Baines, L, & McBrayer, D. *How to get a life.* Atlanta, GA: Humanics, p. 130.

STRATEGY 10

1. National Center for Education Statistics (2021). *Fast facts: Homeschooling.* Washington, DC: U.S. Department of Education. https://nces.ed.gov/fastfacts/display.asp?id=91

2. Eggleston, C., & Fields, J. (2021, March 22). *Census Bureau's household pulse survey shows significant increase in homeschooling rates in fall 2020.* Washington, DC: U.S. Census Bureau. https://www.census.gov/library/stories/2021/03/homeschooling-on-the-rise-during-covid-19-pandemic.html

3. Aikens, N. L., & Barbarin, O. (2008). Socioeconomic differences in reading trajectories: The contribution of family, neighborhood, and school contexts. *Journal of Educational Psychology 100*(2), 235–251.

4. Chetty, R., Friedman, J. N., Hilger, N., Saez, E., Schanzenbach, D. W., & Yagan, D. (2011). How does your kindergarten classroom affect your earnings? Evidence from Project STAR. *The Quarterly Journal of Economics 126*, 1593–1660 (p. 1593).

5. Chetty, R., Friedman, J. N., Hilger, N., Saez, E., Schanzenbach, D. W., & Yagan, D. (2011). How does your kindergarten classroom affect your earnings? Evidence from Project STAR. *The Quarterly Journal of Economics 126*, 1593–1660 (p. 1597).

6. High Scope (2020). *Perry preschool project.* https://highscope.org/perry-preschool-project/; Page, E. B., & Grandon, G. M. (1981). Massive intervention and child intelligence: The Milwaukee project in critical perspective. *The Journal of Special Education 15*(2), 239–256; Campbell, F. A., Pan, Y., & Burchinal, M. (2019). Sustaining gains from early childhood intervention: The Abecedarian program. In A. Reynolds & J. Temple (Eds.), *Sustaining early childhood learning gains: Program, school, and family influences* (pp. 268–286). New York: Cambridge University.

7. Garber, H. (1973). *The Milwaukee Project: Preventing mental retardation in children at risk.* Washington, DC: National Institute of Handicapped Research. https://files.eric.ed.gov/fulltext/ED318183.pdf

8. Yazejian, N., Bryant, D., Kuhn, L., Burchinal, M., Horm, D., Hans, S., File, N., & Jackson, D. (2020). The Educare intervention: Outcomes at age 3, *Early Childhood Research Quarterly 53*, 425–440.

9. Campbell, F. A., Pan, Y., & Burchinal, M. (2019). Sustaining gains from early childhood intervention: The Abecedarian program. In A. Reynolds & J. Temple (Eds.), *Sustaining early childhood learning gains: Program, school, and family influences* (pp. 268–286). New York: Cambridge University.

10. High Scope (2020). *Perry preschool project.* https://highscope.org/perry-preschool-project/; Page, E. B., & Grandon, G. M. (1981). Massive intervention and child intelligence: The Milwaukee project in critical perspective. *The Journal of Special Education 15*(2), 239–256; Campbell, F. A., Pan, Y., & Burchinal, M. (2019). Sustaining gains from early childhood intervention: The Abecedarian program. In A. Reynolds & J. Temple (Eds.), *Sustaining early childhood learning gains: Program, school, and family influences* (pp. 268–286). New York: Cambridge University.

11. Schulte, D., Slate, J., & Onwuegbuzie, A. (2008). Effective high school teachers: A mixed investigation, *International Journal of Educational Research 47*(6), 351–361.

12. Chetty, R., Friedman, J. N., Hilger, N., Saez, E., Schanzenbach, D. W., & Yagan, D. (2011). How does your kindergarten classroom affect your earnings? Evidence from Project STAR. *The Quarterly Journal of Economics 126*, 1593–1660 (pp. 1656–1658).

13. McCoy, D. C., Yoshikawa, H., Ziol-Guest, K. M., Duncan, G. J., Schindler, H. S., Magnuson, K., Yang, R., Koepp, A., & Shonkoff, J. P. (2017). Impacts of early childhood education on medium- and long-term educational outcomes. *Educational Researcher 46*(8), 474–487.

14. Ulferts, H., Wolf, K. M., & Anders, Y. (2019). Impact of process quality in early childhood education and care on academic outcomes: Longitudinal meta-Analysis. *Child Development 90*, 1474–1489.

15. Palardy, G. J., & Rumberger, R. W. (2008). Teacher effectiveness in first grade: The importance of background qualifications, attitudes, and instructional practices for student learning. *Educational Evaluation and Policy Analysis 30*(2), 111–140.

16. Baines, L. A. & Goolsby, R. (2016). America's obsessive assessment disorder. In J. Bowen & P. Thomas (Eds.), *De-testing and de-grading schools* (2nd ed., pp. 64–76). New York: Peter Lang.

17. Nouvelle, C. (2021, November 14). *When a Hyundai is also the family home.* National Public Radio. https://www.npr.org/2021/11/14/1053923521/housing-school-district-pennsylvania-parking-lot

18. U.S. Department of Education (2020). Table 235.20. *Revenues for public elementary and secondary schools, by source of funds and state or jurisdiction: 2016-17.* Washington, DC: National Center for Education Statistics. https://nces.ed.gov/programs/digest/d19/tables/dt19_235.20.asp

19. Brown, C., Sargrad, S., & Benner, M. (2017, April 8). Hidden money: Outsized role of parent contributions in school finance. *Center for American Progress.* https://www.americanprogress.org/issues/education-k-12/reports/2017/04/08/428484/hidden-money/

20. Allen, S. (2020, May 18). Graduation caps year of heartache for Thomas Jefferson seniors. *D Magazine.* https://www.dallasobserver.com/news/graduation-heartache-for-thomas-jefferson-high-school-seniors-11911069

21. Smith, C. (2016, December 9). Texas high school football's latest arms race: multimillion-dollar indoor practice facilities. *Dallas Morning News.* https://www.dallasnews.com/news/education/2016/12/09/texas-high-school-footballs-latest-arms-race-multimillion-dollar-indoor-practice-facilities/

22. Trotter, J. (2011, February 2). Packers impressed with HP practice facility. *CBS Dallas Fort Worth.* https://dfw.cbslocal.com/2011/02/02/packers-impressed-with-hp-practice-facility/

23. Jaramillo, C. (2020, August 10). Violent crime is up in Dallas but city officials at odds on best way to reduce it. *Dallas Morning News.* https://www.dallasnews.com/news/crime/2020/08/10/violent-crime-is-up-in-dallas-but-city-officials-at-odds-on-best-way-to-reduce-it/

24. Wang, K., Chen, Y., Zhang, J., & Oudekerk, B. A. (2020). *Indicators of School Crime and Safety: 2019* (NCES 2020-063/NCJ 254485). Washington, DC: National Center for Education Statistics, U.S. Department of Education, and Bureau of Justice Statistics, Office of Justice Programs, U.S. Department of Justice.

25. See Jiminez, L. (2019). *The case for federal funding for school infrastructure.* Washington, DC: Center for American Progress. Also: Latham, B. (2018, October 15). School infrastructure is in big trouble. Building new schools isn't the answer. *Education Week.* Washington, DC: Editorial Projects in Education. https://www.edweek.org/ew/articles/2018/10/16/school-infrastructure-is-in-big-trouble-building.html

26. National Center of Education Statistics (2020). *Urban schools: The challenge of location and poverty.* Washington, DC: U.S. Department of Education. https://nces.ed.gov/pubs/web/96184ex.asp

27. Barshay, J. (2020, June 8). Rich schools get richer. *Hechinger Report.* https://hechingerreport.org/rich-schools-get-richer/

28. Garcia, E., & Weiss, E. (2019, March 26). The teacher shortage is real, large and growing, and worse than we thought. *Economic Policy Institute.* https://www.epi.org/publication/the-teacher-shortage-is-real-large-and-growing-and-worse-than-we-thought-the-first-report-in-the-perfect-storm-in-the-teacher-labor-market-series/

29. Kelly, M. G. (2020). The curious case of the missing tail: Trends among the top 1% of school districts in the United States, 2000–2015. *Educational Researcher,* 49(5), 312–320.

30. McLaughlin, R. (2016, November 30). *Prop 13: Winners and losers from America's legendary taxpayer revolt.* www.trulia.com/research/prop-13/

31. Redfin (2020). *Palo Alto Housing Market.* www.redfin.com/city/14325/CA/Palo-Alto/housing-market

32. Redfin (2020). *Arvin Housing Market: Home prices in Arvin.* www.redfin.com/city/769/CA/Arvin/housing-market

33. McLaughlin, R. (2016, November 30). *Prop 13: Winners and losers from America's legendary taxpayer revolt.* www.trulia.com/research/prop-13/

34. Vix, B. (2019). The 20 richest cities in Michigan. *Money Inc.* https://moneyinc.com/richest-cities-in-michigan/

35. National Assessment of Educational Progress (2020). *Achievement gaps.* Washington, DC: NAEP. https://nces.ed.gov/nationsreportcard/studies/gaps/

36. Freedberg, L. (2019, November 8). California spending over $13 billion annually on special education. *Edsource.* Oakland, CA: EdSource. https://edsource.org/2019/california-spending-over-13-billion-annually-on-special-education/619542

37. Griffith, M. (2015). A look at funding for students with disabilities. *Education Commission of the States 16*(1). http://www.ecs.org/clearinghouse/01/17/72/11772.pdf

38. Goldhaber, D., Lavery, L., & Theobald, R. (2015). Uneven playing field? Assessing the teacher quality gap between advantaged and disadvantaged students. *Educational Researcher 44*(5), 293–307.

39. Barbarin, O., & Aikens, N. (2015). Overcoming the educational disadvantages of poor children. *American Journal of Orthopsychiatry 85*(2), 101–105. (Citation on p. 104).

40. DiCarlo, M. (2012, March 28). *Ohio's new school rating system.* Washington, DC: Al Shanker Institute. https://www.shankerinstitute.org/blog/ohios-new-school-rating-system-different-results-same-flawed-methods

41. Lowrey, A. (2019, September 13). Her only crime was helping her kids. *The Atlantic.* https://www.theatlantic.com/ideas/archive/2019/09/her-only-crime-was-helping-her-kid/597979/

42. Dolly Madison Community (2011, July 20). Kelly Williams-Bolar is a pathological liar. *Daily Kos.* https://www.dailykos.com/stories/2011/7/20/984388/-

43. Martin, M. (2011), January 28). Mother jailed for school fraud, flares controversy. *All Things Considered.* NPR. https://www.npr.org/2011/01/28/133306180/Mother-Jailed-For-School-Fraud-Flares-Controversy

44. Marshall, A. (2019, January 12). Akron mom's felony convictions for school residency lies reduced to misdemeanors. *The Plain Dealer.* https://www.cleveland.com/open/2011/09/gov_kasich_reduces_felony_conv.html

45. Boston Latin School (2021). *About BLS.* Boston, MA: BLS. https://www.bls.org

46. Gamerman, E. (2007, November 30). How to get into Harvard. *The Wall Street Journal.* https://www.wsj.com/articles/SB119638146482608732

47. National Center for Education Statistics (2020). *Private school enrollment.* Washington, DC: NCES. Nces.ed.gov/programs/coe/indicator_cgc.asp

48. Spiegelman, M. (2020, April 30). New data on public and private school teacher characteristics, experiences, and training. *NCES Blog.* Washington, DC: National Center for Education Statistics. https://nces.ed.gov/blogs/nces/post/new-data-on-public-and-private-school-teacher-characteristics-experiences-and-training

49. National Center for Education Statistics (2005). *Private school teacher turnover and teacher perceptions of school organizational characteristics.* Washington, DC: NCES. https://nces.ed.gov/pubs2005/2005061.pdf

50. Foundations and donors interested in Catholic activities (2020). *Managing governance chance in prek-12 Catholic schools.* Washington, DC: FADICA. https://www.fadica.org/images/initiatives/Managing_Governance_Change_Final_4-6-20.pdf

51. McCluskey, N. (2020, May 29). *Private school COVID-19 permanent closure tracker—May 29, 2020.* Washington, DC: Cato Institute. https://www.cato.org/covid-19-permanent-private-closures

52. National Center for Education Statistics Blog (2020, April 30). *New data on public and private school teacher characteristics, experiences, and training.* Washington, DC: NCES. https://nces.ed.gov/blogs/nces/post/new-data-on-public-and-private-school-teacher-characteristics-experiences-and-training

53. National Center for Education Statistics (2020). *Public and private school comparison.* Washington, DC: NCES. https://nces.ed.gov/fastfacts/display.asp?id=55. Much of the data on the list below derives from this document. Separate endnotes are provided for additional sources of data.

54. Braun, H, Jenkins, F., & Grigg, W. (2006, July). *Comparing private schools and public schools using hierarchical linear modeling.* Washington, DC: National Center for Education Statistics.

55. Woolley, S., & Kazakina, K. (2019, March 27). *At $50,000 a year, 'baby ivies' road to Yale starts at age 5.* New York: Bloomberg. https://www.bloomberg.com/news/articles/2019-03-27/at-50-000-a-year-baby-ivies-road-to-yale-starts-at-age-5

56. Orlin, B. (2013, October 24). Why are private school teachers paid less than public school teachers? *The Atlantic.* https://www.theatlantic.com/education/archive/2013/10/why-are-private-school-teachers-paid-less-than-public-school-teachers/280829/

57. An incredible, but true story. The teacher had been employed by the school for ten years, though she started as a teacher's assistant. See also: Egan, T. (2000, August 6). The changing face of Catholic education. *New York Times.* https://www.nytimes.com/2000/08/06/education/the-changing-face-of-catholic-education.html

58. Baines, L. A. & Machell, J. (2019, November 6). Beware! Money, charters and vouchers. *Tulsa World.* https://www.tulsaworld.com/opinion/columnists/by-lawrence-baines-and-jim-machell-beware-money-charters-and/article_34f29480-6c68-5b23-adb3-36702c738780.html

59. Baines, L. (2019). *Privatization of America's public institutions.* New York: Peter Lang.

60. Graves, L. (2016, April 28). Exposed by CMD: KIPP's efforts to keep the public in the dark while seeking millions in taxpayer subsidies. *PRWatch.* Madison, WI: Center for Media and Democracy. https://www.prwatch.org/news/2016/04/13096/exposed-cmd-kipps-efforts-keep-public-dark-while-seeking-millions-taxpayer. See also: Baines, L. (2019). *Privatization of America's public institutions.* New York: Peter Lang, pp. 88–89.

61. Martinez-Keel, N. (2020, October 13). Epic charter school ordered to pay $11.2 million to state. *The Oklahoman.* https://oklahoman.com/article/5673784/epic-charter-school-ordered-to-pay-112-million-to-the-state

62. Thompson, J. (2019, August 6). How a truly Epic Charter School fraud unfolded in Oklahoma. *The Progressive.* https://progressive.org/public-school-shakedown/embezzling-unregulated-online-charters-thompson-200403/

63. Thompson, J. (2019, August 6). How a truly epic charter school fraud unfolded in Oklahoma. *The Progressive.* https://progressive.org/public-school-shakedown/epic-charter-fraud-oklahoma-thompson-190806/

64. Baines, L. (2019). *Privatization of America's public institutions.* New York: Peter Lang.

65. Burris, C., & Pfeger, R. (2020). *Broken promises: An analysis of charter school closures from 1999–2017*. New York: Network for Public Education. https://networkforpubliceducation.org/brokenpromises/. See p. 6.

66. Burris, C., & Pfeger, R. (2020). *Broken promises: An analysis of charter school closures from 1999–2017*. New York: Network for Public Education. https://networkforpubliceducation.org/brokenpromises/

67. Frankenberg, E., Siegel-Hawley, G, & Wang, J. (2010). *Choice without equity*. Los Angeles, CA: The Civil Rights Project. https://civilrightsproject.ucla.edu/research/k-12-education/integration-and-diversity/choice-without-equity-2009-report

68. Simon, S. (2013, February 15). Special report: Class struggle: How charter schools get students they want. *Reuters*. https://www.reuters.com/article/idUSBRE91E0HF20130215?irpc=932

69. Burris, C., & Pfeger, R. (2020). *Broken promises: An analysis of charter school closures from 1999 – 2017*. New York: Network for Public Education. https://networkforpubliceducation.org/brokenpromises/

70. Ayscue, J., Nelson, A., Mickelson, R., Giersch, J., & Bottia, M. (2018, January 30). *Charters as a driver of resegregation*. Los Angeles, CA: The Civil Rights Project. https://www.civilrightsproject.ucla.edu/research/k-12-education/integration-and-diversity/charters-as-a-driver-of-resegregation

71. Education Commission of the States (2021). *Charter schools: Do teachers have to be certified?* Washington, DC: ECS. http://ecs.force.com/mbdata/MBQuestNB2C?rep=CS2021

72. Niederberger, M. (2017, September 27). *We analyzed teacher salaries at charter schools. Here's what we found*. Pittsburgh, PA: Public Source. https://projects.publicsource.org/chartereffect/stories/we-analyzed-teacher-salaries-at-charter-schools-heres-what-we-found.html. See also: Buhl, L. (2019, June 5). Churn & Burn. *Capital & Main*. https://capitalandmain.com/charter-teachers-challenged-by-working-conditions-lower-pay-0605

73. Education Commission of the States (2021). *What rules are waived for charter schools?* Washington, DC: ECS. http://ecs.force.com/mbdata/MBQuestNB2C?rep=CS2014

74. Prothero, A. (2018, December 20). Charter schools more likely to ignore special education applicants, study finds. *Education Week*. Washington, DC: Editorial Projects in Education. http://ecs.force.com/mbdata/MBQuestNB2C?rep=CS2014

75. Miron, G. (2014). *Charters should be expected to serve all kinds of students*. Cambridge, MA: Education Next. https://www.educationnext.org/charters-expected-serve-kinds-students/

76. Waldman, A. (2017, September 25). Failing charter schools have a reincarnation plan. *Propublica*. New York: ProPublica. https://www.propublica.org/article/failing-charter-schools-have-a-reincarnation-plan

77. Gabor, A. (2019, November). The k-12 takeover. *Harper's*. https://harpers.org/archive/2019/11/the-k-12-takeover-charter-schools-new-orleans/

78. Mannie, S. (2016, August 25). Can Teach for America get more teachers to stick around in some of the nation's poorest schools? *Hechinger Report*. https://

hechingerreport.org/can-teach-for-america-get-more-teachers-to-stick-around-in-some-of-the-nations-poorest-schools/

79. Brewer, J., & deMarrais, K. (Eds.) (2015). *Teach for America counter-narratives.* New York: Peter Lang.

80. Waldman, A. (2019). *How Teach for America evolved into an arm of the charter school movement.* Washington, DC: Propublica. https://www.propublica.org/article/how-teach-for-america-evolved-into-an-arm-of-the-charter-school-movement

81. Brewer, J., & deMarrais, K. (2015). *Teacher for America counter-narratives.* New York: Peter Lang.

STRATEGY 11

1. Chetty, R., Friedman, J., & Rockoff, J. (2011). *The long-term impacts of teachers.* Boston, MA: Harvard University. http://www.rajchetty.com/chettyfiles/value_added.htm

2. Hanushek, E. (2011). The economic value of higher teacher quality. *Economics of Education Review 30*(3), 466–479.

3. Hanushek, E. (2016). *Education and the nation's future.* In George P. Shultz (Ed.), *Blueprint for America.* Stanford, CA: Hoover Institution Press, pp. 89–108.

4. U.S. Department of Education (2020). *The condition of education, 2020.* Washington, DC: U.S. Department of Education.

5. Marzano, R. (2017). *The new art and science of teaching.* Bloomington, IN: Soiution Tree.

6. Piaget, J., & Inhelder, B. (2000). *The psychology of the child.* New York: Basic Books.

7. Csikszentmihalyi, M. (2008). *Flow.* New York: Harper.

8. This free file from Wiki Commons illustrates the difficulty of creating academic tasks that are equal to a student's ability. The graphic is derived from descriptions of flow found in Csikszentmihalyi, M. (2008). *Flow.* New York: Harper.

9. Vygotsky, L. (1980). *Mind in society.* Cambridge, MA: Harvard University Press.

10. Greenberg, M. T., Brown J. L., & Abenavoli, R. M. (2016). *Teacher stress and health effects on teachers, students, and schools.* Edna Bennett Pierce Prevention Research Center, Pennsylvania State University. https://www.rwjf.org/en/library/research/2016/07/teacher-stress-and-health.html

11. de Souza, J. C., de Sousa, I. C., Belísio, A. S., & de Azevedo, C. V. M. (2012). Sleep habits, daytime sleepiness and sleep quality of high school teachers. *Psychology & Neuroscience 2,* 257–263.

12. See: Borko, H., & Shavelson, R. (1990). Teacher decision making. In B. Jones & L. Idol (Eds.), *Dimensions of thinking and cognitive instruction* (pp. 311–346); Danielson, C. (1996). *Enhancing professional practice: A framework for teaching.* Alexandria, VA: Association for Supervision and Curriculum Development; Jackson, P. (1990), *Life in classrooms.* New York: Teachers College Press. In 2020, a group called Busy Teacher postulated that teachers made 1,500 decisions every day, but the methodology for arriving at this number was not apparent.

13. Bureau of Labor Statistics (2020). *Occupational Handbook*. Washington, DC: Bureau of Labor Statistics. https://www.bls.gov/ooh/education-training-and-library/high-school-teachers.htm

14. Csikszentmihalyi, M. (1997). *Finding flow*. New York: Basic Books.

15. McCarthy, C. (2019, Oct. 28). Teacher stress: Balancing demands and resources. *Phi Delta Kappan 101*(3), 8–14.

16. A version of this story has previously appeared in Oklahoma City's newspaper, *The Oklahoman*. Baines, L. A. (2016, January 6). Effective teachers make an incredible difference. *The Oklahoman*, 13A.

17. National Institute of Neurological Disorders and Stroke (2021). *Asperger Syndrome information page*. https://www.ninds.nih.gov/Disorders/All-Disorders/Asperger-Syndrome-Information-Page

18. Bloom, B., Engelhart, M., Furst, E., Hill, W., & Krathwohl, D. (1956). Taxonomy of educational objectives: The classification of educational goals. *Handbook I: Cognitive domain*. New York: David McKay Company.

19. Bloom. B. (1984). The two sigma problem. *Educational Researcher 13*(6), 4–16.

20. Waxman, H., & Walberg, H. (1986). Teaching and productivity. *Education and Urban Society 18*(2), 211–220.

21. Bloom. B. (1984). The two sigma problem. *Educational Researcher 13*(6), 4–16.

22. Jackson, K. (2018). What do test scores miss? The importance of teacher effects on non-test score outcomes. *Journal of Political Economy 126*(5), 2072–2107; Kautz, T., Heckman, J., Diris, R., Weel, Bas ter, & Borghans, L. (2017). *Fostering and measuring skills: Improving cognitive and non-cognitive skills to promote lifetime success*. National Bureau of Economic Research Working Paper No. 20749. Cambridge, MA: NBER. https://www.nber.org/papers/w20749; Heckman, J., Stixrud, J., & Urzua, S. (2006). The effects of cognitive and noncognitive abilities on labor market outcomes and social behavior. National Bureau of Economic Research Working Paper No. 12006. Cambridge, MA: NBER. http://www.nber.org/papers/w12006

23. Jedd, K., Hunt, R., Cicchetti, D., Hunt, E., Cowell, R., Rogosch, F., Toth, S. & Thomas, K. (2015). Long-term consequences of childhood maltreatment: Altered amygdala functional connectivity. *Development and Psychopathology 27*, 1577–1589 (citation on p. 1577).

24. Cacioppo, J. T., & Patrick, W. (2008). *Loneliness: Human nature and the need for social connection*. New York: W. W. Norton.

25. Holt-Lunstad, J., Smith, T. B., Baker, M., Harris, T., & Stephenson, D. (2015). Loneliness and social isolation as risk factors for mortality: a meta-analytic review. *Perspectives on psychological science: a journal of the Association for Psychological Science 10*(2), 227–237. Citation on p. 227.

26. Ladson-Billings, G. (1994). *The dreamkeepers*. San Francisco, CA: Jossey-Bass; see also Noddings, N. (2003). *Happiness and education*. New York: Cambridge University Press.

27. Groark, C., McCall, R., & Fish, L. (2011). Characteristics of environments, caregivers, and children in three Central American orphanages. *Infant Mental Health Journal 32*(2), 232–250.

28. Centers for Disease Control and Prevention (2020). *Early brain development and health.* Washington, DC: CDC. https://www.cdc.gov/ncbddd/childdevelopment/early-brain-development.html

29. Greene, M. (2020). 30 years ago, Romania deprived thousands of babies of human contact: What's become of them? *The Atlantic.* https://www.theatlantic.com/magazine/archive/2020/07/can-an-unloved-child-learn-to-love/612253/

30. Weissbourd, R., & Anderson, T. (2016, March). Do we value caring? *Educational Leadership,* 54–58.

31. Merriam-Webster Dictionary. *Definition of apathy.* https://www.merriam-webster.com/dictionary/apathy

32. Hodges, T. (2018, October 25). School engagement is more than just talk. *Gallup.* Washington, DC: Gallup. https://www.gallup.com/education/244022/school-engagement-talk.aspx

33. Wise, S. L. (2019, Oct. 28). The emerging science of test-taking disengagement. *Phi Delta Kappan 101*(3), 72.

34. Patrick, B. C., Hisley, J., & Kempler, T. (2000). "What's everybody so excited about?": The effects of teacher enthusiasm on student intrinsic motivation and vitality. *The Journal of Experimental Education 68*(3), 217–236. Citation on p. 217.

35. Parry, J. (1953, September). Self through service. *The Rotarian,* p. 6.

36. Keller, M. M., Hoy, A. W., Goetz, T., & Frenzel, A. C. (2016). Teacher enthusiasm: Reviewing and redefining a complex construct. *Educational Psychology Review 28*(4), 743–769.

37. Keller, M. M., Hoy, A. W., Goetz, T., & Frenzel, A. C. (2016). Teacher enthusiasm: Reviewing and redefining a complex construct. *Educational Psychology Review 28*(4), 743–769.

38. Patrick, B. C., Hisley, J., & Kempler, T. (2000). "What's everybody so excited about?": The effects of teacher enthusiasm on student intrinsic motivation and vitality. *The Journal of Experimental Education 68*(3), 217–236. Citation on p. 217.

39. Zhang, Q. (2014). Assessing the effects of instructor enthusiasm on classroom engagement, learning goal orientation, and academic self-efficacy. *Communication Teacher 28*(1), 44–56. Citation on p. 44.

40. Marlin, J. (1991). State-mandated economic education, teacher attitudes, and student learning. *Journal of Economic Education 22,* 5–14.

41. Patrick, B., Hisley, J., & Kempler, T. (2000). What's everybody so excited about? The effects of teacher enthusiasm on student intrinsic motivation and vitality. *Journal of Experiential Education 68,* 217–236

42. Frenzel, A. C., Goetz, T., Lüdtke, O., Pekrun, R., & Sutton, R. E. (2009). Emotional transmission in the classroom: Exploring the relationship between teacher and student enjoyment. *Journal of Educational Psychology 101*(3), 705.

43. Jungert, T., Levine, S., & Koestner, R. (2020). Examining how parent and teacher enthusiasm influences motivation and achievement in STEM. *The Journal of Educational Research 113*(4), 275–282.

44. Kunter, M., Frenzel, A., Nagy, G., Baumert, J., & Pekrun, R. (2011). Teacher enthusiasm: Dimensionality and context specificity. *Contemporary Educational Psychology, 36*(4), 289–301.

45. Douglas, E. (2012, March 28). Monetary vs. nonmonetary rewards: Which are more attractive? *Education Week.* https://www.edweek.org/leadership/opinion-monetary-vs-non-monetary-rewards-which-are-more-attractive/2012/03

46. Smedes, L. (1991). *On being truthful.* Wheaton, IL: Center for Applied Christian Ethics. https://www.wheaton.edu/media/migrated-images-amp-files/media/files/centers-and-institutes/cace/booklets/BeingTruthful.pdf

47. Wisniewski, B., Zierer, K., & Hattie, J. (2020) The power of feedback revisited: A meta-analysis of educational feedback research. *Frontiers in Psychology 10*, 3087. https://www.frontiersin.org/articles/10.3389/fpsyg.2019.03087/full

48. Doyle, W. (1983). Academic work. *Review of Educational Research 53*(2), 159–199.

49. Butler, D., & Winne, P. (1995). Feedback and self-regulated learning: A theoretical synthesis. *Review of Educational Research 65*(3), 245–281.

50. Stanley, G. S., & Baines, L. A. (2002, Winter). Celebrating mediocrity: How schools shortchange gifted students. *Roeper Review*, 11–13.

51. Brophy. J. (1981). Teacher praise: A functional analysis. *Review of Educational Research 51*, 5–32.

52. Xu, Y., & Carless, D. (2017). "Only true friends could be cruelly honest": cognitive scaffolding and social-effective support in teacher feedback literacy. *Assessment & Evaluation in Higher Education 42*(7), 1082–1094.

53. Hattie, J., & Timperley, H. (2007). The power of feedback. *Review of Educational Research 77*(1), 81–112.

54. Heick, T. (2013). New reasons to dislike multiple-choice testing. *Edutopia.* https://www.edutopia.org/blog/reasons-to-dislike-multi-choice-terrell-heick

55. Fair Test (2007). *Multiple-choice tests.* Arlington, MA: Fair test. https://www.fairtest.org/multiple-choice-tests

56. Argyropoulou, E. (2020). Lying in the teaching profession. *International Journal of Ethics & Education 5*, 243–259.

57. Jefferson, T. (2021, c1819). *Letter to Nathaniel Macon, January 12, 1819.* Washington, DC: Library of Congress. https://www.loc.gov/resource/mtj1.051_0212_0213/

58. Ravitch, D. (2003). *A brief history of teacher professionalism.* U.S. Department of Education White House Conference on Preparing Tomorrow's Teachers. Washington, DC: U.S. Department of Education. https://www2.ed.gov/admins/tchrqual/learn/preparingteachersconference/ravitch.html

59. Baines, L. A. (2010). *The teachers we need, the teachers we have.* Lanham, MD: Rowman & Littlefield.

60. American Board for Certification of Teacher Excellence (2020). *Ohio teacher certification.* Atlanta, GA: ABCTE. https://www.americanboard.org/ohio/.

61. Ohio laws and rules (2020). Chapter 3301: Department of Education. Columbus, OH: Ohio Laws and Rules. http://codes.ohio.gov/orc/3301

62. Tuttle, C., Anderson, T., & Glazerman, S. (2009). *ABCTE teachers in Florida and their effect on student performance*. Washington, DC: Mathematica Policy Institute. https://www.mathematica.org/publications/abcte-teachers-in-florida-and-their-effect-on-student-performance

63. See http://www.texasteachers.org

64. The Texas Title 2 Report, "State enrollment information" at https://title2.ed.gov/Public/Report/StateHighlights/StateHighlights.aspx?p=2_01.

65. The National Center for Teacher Quality has notoriously low standards. However, even NCTQ gave Texas Teachers an F in everything. See https://www.nctq.org/review/view/Texas-Teachers-(formerly-known-as-A-Texas-Teachers)-TX-4

66. Baines, L. A. (2010). *The teachers we need, the teachers we have*. Lanham, MD: Rowman & Littlefield.

67. Baines, L. A. (2019). *Privatizing America's public institutions: The story of the American sellout*. New York: Peter Lang.

68. National Conference of State Legislatures (2016). *No time to lose*. Washington, DC: NCSL. http://www.ncsl.org/documents/educ/EDU_International_final_v3.pdf

69. Barrera-Pedemonte, F. (2016). High-quality teacher professional development and classroom teaching practices: Evidence from Talis 2013. OECD Education Working Papers, No. 141. Paris: OECD Publishing. http://dx.doi.org/10.1787/5jlpszw26rvd-en; OECD (2012), *Equity and quality in education: Supporting disadvantaged students and schools*, OECD Publishing. http://dx.doi.org/10.1787/9789264130852-en

70. Mann, H. (1848). *Report No. 12 of the Massachusetts School Board*. Boston, MA: Masschusetts Department of Edcuation.

71. Rice, J. (2003). *Teacher quality*. Washington, DC: Economic Policy Institute.

72. Opper, I. (2019). *Teachers matter*. Santa Monica, CA: Rand Corporation.

73. Texas Education Agency (2020). *SBEC disciplinary action reports*. Austin, TX. https://tea.texas.gov/texas-educators/investigations/disciplinary-actions-taken-against-texas-educators. See also: Chang, J. (2016, September 21). Cases of improper teacher-student relationships hit 8-year high. *Austin American Statesman*. http://www.mystatesman.com/news/state--regional-govt--politics/cases-improper-teacher-student-relationships-hit-year-high/UE0uA8f83tzJGHNrp5GkwO/

74. Chang, J. (2018, November 27). Number of teacher misconduct cases rises for 10th year in a row. *Austin American Statesman*. https://www.statesman.com/news/20181127/number-of-teacher-misconduct-cases-rises-for-10th-year-in-row

75. Texas Education Agency (2021). *Disciplinary actions taken against Texas educators*. https://tea.texas.gov/texas-educators/investigations/disciplinary-actions-taken-against-texas-educators

76. Ramirez, M. (2017, August 4). *Dallas Morning News*. Former Dallas teacher sentenced to 40 years for sexually assaulting students. https://www.dallasnews.com/news/crime/2017/08/05/former-dallas-teacher-sentenced-to-40-years-for-sexually-assaulting-students/

77. See the College Board Program Results for Texas at https://www.collegeboard.org/program-results/2014/texas

STRATEGY 12

1. Rock, D. & Pollack, J. (1995). *The relationship between gains in achievement in mathematics and selected course taking behaviors*. Washington, DC: National Center for Education Statistics.

2. Iatarola, P. (2016). Implications for scaling up advanced course offerings and takings: Evidence from Florida. *Teachers College Record 118*(13). https://www.tcrecord.org/Content.asp?ContentId=20556

3. National Association for Gifted Children (2021). *How much does the federal government spend on gifted education?* Washington, DC: NAGC. https://www.nagc.org/resources-publications/resources/frequently-asked-questions-about-gifted-education

4. U.S. Department of Education Office of Elementary and Secondary Education (2021). *Jacob K. Javits Gifted and Talented Students Education Program*. Washington, DC: U.S. Department of Education. https://oese.ed.gov/offices/office-of-discretionary-grants-support-services/well-rounded-education-programs/jacob-k-javits-gifted-and-talented-students-education-program/

5. U.S. Census Bureau (2020). *Spending per pupil increased for sixth consecutive year*. Washington, DC: U.S. Census Bureau. https://www.census.gov/newsroom/press-releases/2020/school-system-finances.html. Also see American Association of School Administrators (2009). *School budgets 101*. Alexandria, VA: AASA. https://www.aasa.org/uploadedfiles/policy_and_advocacy/files/schoolbudgetbrieffinal.pdf

6. National Association for Gifted Children (2020). *State of the states in gifted education*. Washington, DC: NAGC.

7. Loveless, T. (2013). *How well are American students learning?* Washington, DC: Brookings Institute.

8. Nevada System of Higher Education (2012, November). *Remedial transformation project*. Las Vegas, NV: NSHE.

9. National Association for Gifted Children (2021). *A definition of giftedness that guides best practice*. Washington, DC: NAGC. https://www.nagc.org/sites/default/files/Position%20Statement/Definition%20of%20Giftedness%20%282019%29.pdf

10. Lubinski, D., & Benbow, C. (2021). Intellectual precocity: What have we learned since Terman? *Gifted Child Quarterly 65*(1), 3–28.

11. Clynes, T. (2016, September). How to raise a genius. *Nature 537*, 152–156.

12. Radford, J. (1990). *Child prodigies and exceptional early learners*. New York: The Free Press. Citation on p. 207.

13. Baines, L. A., & Stanley, G. K. (2003, Summer). Disengagement and loathing in high school. *Educational Horizons*, 165–168.

14. Brookhart, S. M., Walsh, J., & Zientarski, W. (2006). The dynamics of motivation and effort for classroom assessments in middle school science and social studies. *Applied Measurement in Education 19*, 151–184.

15. Long, B., & Boatman, A. (2013). The role of remedial and developmental courses in access and persistence. In A. Jones & L. Perna (Eds.), *The state of college access and completion* (pp. 77–96). New York: Routledge.

16. Milewski, G., & Gillie, J. (2002). *What are the characteristics of AP Teachers?* New York: The College Board.

17. Paek, P., Ponte, E., Sigel, I., Braun, H., & Powers, D. (2005). *A portrait of Advanced Placement teachers' practices*. New York: College Board.

18. Bausmith, J., & Laitusis, V. (2012). *The impact of AP Achievement Institute I on students' AP performance*. New York: College Board.

19. Haney, W. (1981). Validity, vaudeville, and values: A short history of social concerns over standardized testing. *American Psychologist 36*(10), 1021–1034.

20. Baines, L. A. & Goolsby, R. (2016). America's obsessive assessment disorder. In J. Bowen & P. Thomas (Eds.), *De-testing and de-grading schools* (second edition, pp. 64–76). New York: Peter Lang.

21. Baines, L. A., & Stanley, G. K. (2004, Fall). High stakes hustle: Public schools and the new, billion dollar accountability. *Educational Forum*, 8–15.

22. Bauer-Wolf, J. (2020, June 30). Is this the end for college admissions tests? *Higher ed dive*. https://www.highereddive.com/news/is-this-the-end-for-college-admissions-tests/580548/

23. College Board (2021). *8 things to know about how colleges use admission tests*. New York: College Board. https://bigfuture.collegeboard.org/get-in/testing/8-things-to-know-about-how-colleges-use-admission-tests

24. Brondo Davidoff, J. (2014, December 15). The SAT is meaningless because it's so easy to game. *Quartz*. https://qz.com/305836/the-sat-is-meaningless-because-its-so-easy-to-game/

STRATEGY 13

1. National Federation of State High School Associations (2020). *The case for high school activities*. Indianapolis, IN: NFSHSA. www.hfhs.org/articles/the-case-for-high-school-activities

2. Maslen, P. (2015, December 29). The social and academic benefits of team sports. Edutopia. www.edutopia.org/discussion/social-and-academic-benefits-team-sports

3. Physical Activity Council (2019). *2020 Physical Activity Council's overview report on U.S. participation*. Jupiter, FL: Sports Marketing Surveys. www.physicalactivitycouncil.com

4. Middlebook, H. (2020). The case for running high mileage in high school. *Runner's World*. https://www.runnersworld.com/training/a32346921/benefits-of-running-high-mileage-in-high-school/

5. American Academy of Pediatrics (2020). *Is your child ready for sports?* Chicago, IL: AAP. www.aap.org

6. American Academy of Pediatrics (2020). *Is your child ready for sports?* Chicago, IL: AAP. www.aap.org

7. National Athletic Trainers Association (2020). *The benefits of high school and youth sports*. Carrollton, TX: NATA. www.atyourworkrisk.org

8. Deelen, I., Ettema, D., & Kamphuis C. (2018). Sports participation in sport clubs, gyms or public spaces: How users of different sports settings differ in their motivations, goals, and sports frequency. *PLoS ONE 13*(10), e0205198.

9. Ronkainen, N., & Ryba, T. (2020) Developing narrative identities in youth pre-elite sport: bridging the present and the future, *Qualitative Research in Sport, Exercise and Health 12*(4), 548–562.

10. Howie, E., & Pate, R. (2012). Physical activity and academic achievement in children: A historical perspective. *Journal of Sport and Health Science 1*(3), 160–169.

11. Raglin, J. (1990). Exercise and mental health. *Sports Medicine 9*(6), 323–329.

12. Moeijs, J., van Busschbach, J., Wieringa, T., Kone, J., Bosscher, R., & Twisk, J. (2019). Sports participation and health-related quality of life in children: results of a cross-sectional study. *Health Quality of Life Outcomes 17*(64).

13. Bowker, A. (2006). The relationship between sports participation and self-esteem during early adolescence. *Canadian Journal of Behavioural Science 38*(3), 214–229.

14. Hickey, W. (2014, May 11). Why cheerleading ranks in safety among high school sports. *FiveThirtyEight*. https://fivethirtyeight.com/features/cheerleading-safety-high-school-sports/

15. Currie, D., Fields, S., Patterson, M., & Comstock, R. (2016, January). Cheerleading injuries in United States high schools. *Pediatrics 137*(1), 2015–2447.

16. Comstock, R. D., & Pierpoint, L. (2019). *Summary report: National high school sports-related injury surveillance study, 2018-2019 school year*. Aurora, CO: Colorado School of Public Health. https://coloradosph.cuanschutz.edu/docs/librariesprovider204/default-document-library/2018-19.pdf?sfvrsn=d26400b9_2

17. Belanger, H. G., & Vanderploeg, R. D. (2005). The neuropsychological impact of sports-related concussion: a meta-analysis. *Journal of the International Neuropsychological Society 11*(4), 345–357.

18. Spring, B., Brooks, A., & Winograd, S. (2019). *Sports-related concussion* (monograph). Morrisville, NC: Relias media. www.reliasmedia.com

19. Spring, B., Brooks, A., & Winograd, S. (2019). *Sports-related concussion* (monograph). Morrisville, NC: Relias media. www.reliasmedia.com. See also: American Academy of Pediatrics (2011). *Policy statement—Boxing participation by children and adolescents*. Chicago, IL: AAP. www.pediatrics.aapublications.org

20. Montenigro, P. H., Corp, D. T., Stein, T. D., Cantu, R. C., & Stern, R. A. (2015). Chronic traumatic encephalopathy: Historical origins and current perspective. *Annual Review of Clinical Psychology 11*, 309–330.

21. Mez, J., Daneshvar, D. H., Kiernan, P. T., Abdolmohammadi, B., Alvarez, V. E., Huber, B. R., Alosco, M. L., Solomon, T. M., Nowinski, C. J., McHale, L., Cormier, K. A., Kubilus, C. A., Martin, B. M., Murphy, L., Baugh, C. M., Montenigro, P. H., Chaisson, C. E., Tripodis, Y., Kowall, N. W., Weuve, J., & McKee, A. C. (2017). Clinicopathological evaluation of Chronic Traumatic Encephalopathy in players of American football. *JAMA 318*(4), 360–370. https://doi.org/10.1001/jama.2017.8334

22. Mez, J., Daneshvar, D. H., Kiernan, P. T., Abdolmohammadi, B., Alvarez, V. E., Huber, B. R., Alosco, M. L., Solomon, T. M., Nowinski, C. J., McHale, L., Cormier, K. A., Kubilus, C. A., Martin, B. M., Murphy, L., Baugh, C. M., Montenigro, P. H.,

Chaisson, C. E., Tripodis, Y., Kowall, N. W., Weuve, J., & McKee, A. C. (2017). Clinicopathological evaluation of Chronic Traumatic Encephalopathy in players of American football. *JAMA 318*(4), 360–370. https://doi.org/10.1001/jama.2017.8334

23. Comstock, R. D., & Pierpoint, L. (2019). *Summary report: National high school sports-related injury surveillance study, 2018-2019 school year*. Aurora, CO: Colorado School of Public Health. https://coloradosph.cuanschutz.edu/docs/librariesprovider204/default-document-library/2018-19.pdf?sfvrsn=d26400b9_2

24. National College Athletic Association (2021). *Scholarships*. https://www.ncaa.org/student-athletes/future/scholarships

25. National Collegiate Athletic Association (2021). *Facts about NCAA sports*. https://www.nfhs.org/media/886012/recruiting-fact-sheet-web.pdf

26. Georgia State University (2006). *From high school to pro: How many will go?* Atlanta, GA: Georgia Career Information Center. https://whenyoucantgopro.weebly.com/uploads/2/6/5/2/26529572/from_high_school_to_pro_statistics.pdf

STRATEGY 14

1. Goldstein, D. (2019, October 25). What do striking teachers want? More counselor's more nurses. *New York Times*, A12.

2. Willgerodt, M. A., Brock, D. M., & Maughan, E. M. (2018). Public school nursing practice in the United States. *The Journal of School Nursing 34*(3), 232–244; Camera, L. (2016, March 23). Many school districts don't have enough school nurses. *U.S. World and News Report*. https://www.usnews.com/news/articles/2016-03-23/the-school-nurse-shortage; Durant, B. V., Gibbons, L. J., Poole, C., Suessmanm, M., & Wyckoff, L. (2011). NASN position statement: caseload assignments. *NASN School Nurse 26*(1), 49–51.

3. Willgerodt, M. A., Brock, D. M., & Maughan, E. M. (2018). Public school nursing practice in the United States. *The Journal of School Nursing 34*(3), 232–244.

4. National Center for Education Statistics (2020). *School and staffing survey: Average FTE nurses in schools and ratio of students to FTE nurses in schools with at least one nurse, by school type and selected school characteristics: 2007–08 and 2011–12*. Washington, DC: U.S. Department of Education. https://nces.ed.gov/surveys/sass/tables/sass1112_20161115001_s12n.asp

5. Juszczak, L., Melinkovich, P., & Kaplan, D. (2003). Use of health and mental health services by adolescents across multiple delivery sites. *The Journal of Adolescent Health 32*(6), 108–118.

6. National Center for Education Statistics (2020). *Digest of Education Statistics 2019*. Washington, DC: NCES. Citation from p. 57.

7. American Association of School Librarians (2016). *Appropriate staffing for school libraries*. Washington, DC: AASL. www.ala.org

8. National Center for Education Statistics (2020). *Table 701.10 Selected statistics on public school library/media centers, by level of school*. Washington, DC: NCES. www.nces.ed.gov

9. California Department of Education (2020). *School libraries: Staffing.* Sacramento, CA: California Department of Education. https://www.cde.ca.gov/ci/cr/cf/cefschoollibraries.asp

10. National Center for Education Statistics (2020). *Table 213.20.Staff employed in public elementary and secondary school systems, by type of assignment and state or jurisdiction: Fall 2017.* Washington, DC: U.S. Department of Education. https://nces.ed.gov/programs/digest/d19/tables/dt19_213.20.asp

11. Chandler, M. (2015, March 10). Charter schools less likely to have libraries. *Washington Post.* https://www.washingtonpost.com/local/education/charter-schools-less-likely-to-have-libraries/2015/03/10/5e5e723a-c739-11e4-b2a1-bed1aaea2816_story.html

12. Levin, K. (2019, August 8). Amid a literacy crisis, Michigan's school librarians have all but disappeared. *Chalkbeat.* https://detroit.chalkbeat.org/2019/8/8/21108625/amid-a-literacy-crisis-michigan-s-school-librarians-have-all-but-disappeared

13. Maughan, S. (2020, August 14). Supporting school librarians through Covid-19 and beyond. *Publishers Weekly.* https://www.publishersweekly.com/pw/by-topic/childrens/childrens-industry-news/article/84105-supporting-school-librarians-through-covid-19-and-beyond.html

14. Yorio, K. (2020, April 2). School librarians can help during crisis, but some fear being shut out. *School Library Journal.* https://www.slj.com/?detailStory=school-librarians-can-help-during-crisis-but-some-fear-being-shut-out-coronavirus-covid19

15. Dorn, E., Hancock, B., Sarakatsannis, J., & Viruleg, E. (2020, June 1). *COVID-19 and student learning in the United States: The hurt could last a lifetime.* New York: McKinsey and Company.

16. American Association of School Librarians (2014). *Causality: School libraries and student success.* Washington, DC: AASL. http://www.ala.org/aasl/sites/ala.org.aasl/files/content/advocacy/research/docs/CLASSWhitePaper_FINAL.pdf

17. California Department of Education (2020). *The importance of school libraries.* Sacramento, CA: California Department of Education. https://www.cde.ca.gov/ci/cr/cf/cefschoollibraries.asp

18. Hanna, J. (2019, Fall). Outnumbered. *Harvard Education Magazine.* Cambridge, MA: Harvard University. https://www.gse.harvard.edu/news/ed/19/08/outnumbered

19. Kolodinsky, P., Draves, P., Schroder, V., Lindsey, C., & Zlatev, M. (2009). Reported levels of satisfaction and frustration by Arizona school counselors: A desire for greater connections with students in a data-driven era. *Professional School Counseling 12*(3), 193–199.

20. Center for Disease Control and Prevention (2020). *Facts about mental disorders in U.S. children.* Washington, DC: CDC. https://www.cdc.gov/childrensmentalhealth/data.html

21. Ghandour, R., Sherman, L, Vladutiu, C., Mir, M., Lynch, S., Bitsko, R., & Blumberg, S. (2019, March 1). Prevalence and treatment of depression, anxiety, and conduct problems in US children. *The Journal of Pediatrics 206*, 256–267. https://www.jpeds.com/article/S0022-3476(18)31292-7/fulltext

22. Viorst, J. (1987). *Alexander and the terrible, horrible, no good, very bad day.* New York: Aladdin.

23. American School Counselor Association (2020). *Student to counselor ratio.* Alexandria, VA: ASCA. https://www.schoolcounselor.org/asca/media/asca/home/Ratios18-19.pdf

24. Whitaker, A., Torres-Guillen, S., Morton, M., Jordan, H., Coyle, S., Mann, A., & Sun, W. (2019). *Cops and no counselors.* New York: ACLU.

25. Whitaker, A., Torres-Guillen, S., Morton, M., Jordan, H., Coyle, S., Mann, A., & Sun, W. (2019). *Cops and no counselors.* New York: ACLU.

26. Whitaker, A., Torres-Guillen, S., Morton, M., Jordan, H., Coyle, S., Mann, A., & Sun, W. (2019). *Cops and no counselors.* New York: ACLU.

27. Savitz-Romer, M., Nicola, T., Jensen, A., Hill, N., Liang, B., & Perella, J. (2019). Data-driven school counseling: The role of the research-practice partnership. *Professional School Counseling 22*(1): 1–9 (citation from p. 2).

28. National Association for College Admission Counseling (2017). *2017 State of college admission.* Alexandria, VA: ASCA. https://www.schoolcounselor.org/About-School-Counseling/School-Counselor-Roles-Ratios

29. American School Counselor Association. (2012). *The ASCA National Model: A framework for school counseling programs* (3rd ed.). Alexandria, VA: ASCA, p. 25.

STRATEGY 15

1. Ming, L, Gilbert, L., Tam, V., Chiu, H., Li, S., & Sin, K. (2020). Parents' impact on children's school performance. *Journal of Child & Family Studies 29*(6), 1548–1560.

2. Ghang, J., Savla, J., & Cheng, H. (2019). Cumulative risk and immigrant youth's health and educational achievement: Mediating effects of inter- and intra-familial social capital. *Youth & Society 51*(6), 793–813.

3. Chua, A. (2011). *Battle hymn of the Tiger Mom.* New York: Penguin.

4. Wong, R., Ho, F., Wong, W., Tung, K., Chow, C., Rao, N., Chan, K., Ip, P. (2018). Parental involvement in primary school education. *Journal of Child and Family Studies 27*, 1544–1555.

5. Brajsa-Zganec, A., Merkas, M., & Sakic Velic, M. (2019). The relations of parental supervision, parental school involvement, and child's social competence with school achievement in primary school. *Psychology in the Schools 56*, 1246–1258. Citation on p. 1253.

6. Fehrmann, P., Keith, T., & Reimers, T. (1987). Home influence on school learning: Direct and indirect effects of parental involvement on high school grades. *Journal of educational research 80*(6), 330–337.

7. McWayne, C., Hampton, V., Fantuzzo, J., Cohen, H., & Sekino, Y. (2004). A multivariate examination of parent involvement and the social and academic competencies of urban kindergarten children. *Psychology in the Schools 41*(3), 363–377.

8. McWayne, C., Hampton, V., Fantuzzo, J., Cohen, H., & Sekino, Y. (2004). A multivariate examination of parent involvement and the social and academic competencies of urban kindergarten children. *Psychology in the Schools 41*(3), 363–377.

9. Cabus, S., & Aries, R. (2017). What do parents teach their children? *Educational Review 69*(3), 285–302. Citation from page 296.

10. Lamb, M. (2010). *The role of the father in child development.* Hoboken, NJ: Wiley.

11. U.S. Department of Education (2000). *A call to commitment: Fathers' involvement in children's learning.* Washington, DC: U.S. Department of Education. https://www2.ed.gov/pubs/parents/calltocommit/fathers.pdf

12. Baker, T., Campbell, S., & Ostroff, D. (2015). *Independent school leadership.* Nashville, TN: Peabody College at Vanderbilt.

13. Wallace Foundation (2013). *The school principal as leader.* New York: The Wallace Foundation.

14. Roosevelt Public Schools (2021). *Chief school administrator appointment, job description and job evaluation.* Roosevelt, New Jersey: Roosevelt Public Schools. http://www.rps1.org/policies/2000/2131%20Chief%20School%20Administrator%20Appointment%20Job%20Description%20and%20Job%20Evaluation.pdf

15. Klocko, B., & Wells, C. (2015). Workload pressures of principals. *NASSP Bulletin 99*(4), 332–355.

16. Coll, C., Akiba, D., Palacios, N., Bailey, B., Silver, R., DiMartino, L, & Chin, C. (2002) Parental involvement in children's education: Lessons from three immigrant groups, *Parenting 2*(3), 303–324

17. Braudy, S. (1977, August 21). He's Woody Allen's not-so-silent partner, *New York Times*, p. 83.

About the Author

Lawrence Baines earned his PhD from the University of Texas at Austin and is currently the director of teacher education at Berry College. He is a former K–12 public school teacher who has worked and consulted in over one thousand schools. *How to Give Your Child the Best Education* is his thirteenth book.

www.ingramcontent.com/pod-product-compliance
Lightning Source LLC
Chambersburg PA
CBHW020125240426
43673CB00038B/603